7-1   1500

The Patient and the Analyst
The Basis of the Psychoanalytic Process

The Patient and the Analyst

The Basis of the Psychoanalytic Process

JOSEPH SANDLER M.A., M.D., D.Sc., Ph.D.

CHRISTOPHER DARE B.A., M.B., B.Chir., M.R.C.P.,
D.P.M., M.R.C.Psych.

ALEX HOLDER D. Phil.

International Universities Press, Inc.
New York

© Joseph Sandler 1973

Published in the U.S.A. by International Universities Press, Inc.
239 Park Avenue South, New York, N.Y. 10003

Library of Congress Catalog Card Number: 73-7023
ISBN 0-8236-4030-2

Second Printing, 1974

Preface

Some three years ago we began an intensive research study on basic psychoanalytic concepts. This was felt to be necessary because of the difficulties we had encountered in teaching psychoanalytic theory to intelligent postgraduate students of psychiatry, a difficulty which we had realized was due, in no small part, to a lack of clarity in the concepts themselves. Fortunately, the clarification of certain basic ideas was a research task appropriate to our role in the Institute of Psychiatry. This book presents the results of our work in a form which we hope will make the basic clinical concepts of psychoanalysis clearer in their meaning and development. We also believe that it may provide the basis for the adequate and appropriate extension of psychoanalytic concepts to related fields, such as those of psychoanalytically orientated psychotherapy and casework. We hope that this book can help dispel some of the mystique still surrounding psychoanalytic ideas. As students and teachers of psychoanalysis we found, in the course of this work, that our own thinking in this area had been substantially clarified and in many respects modified. It is our hope that this book will be of particular value to those training at and teaching in psychoanalytic training institutes.

We are indebted to Sir Denis Hill, Professor of Psychiatry at the Institute of Psychiatry, for the special efforts which he made to provide us with the opportunity and facilities to carry out our work, and for his continued encouragement. Dr Eliot Slater risked his reputation as Editor-in-Chief of *The British Journal of Psychiatry* in accepting a series of ten papers* containing much of the work included in this book after seeing only the first two, and we are grateful to him for this, as for his tolerant and good-humoured support.

* Sandler, Dare and Holder, 1970a, b, c, d, 1971; Sandler, Holder and Dare, 1970a, b, c, d, e. Some additional material has been drawn from two other papers (Sandler, 1968, 1969).

7

A number of colleagues, in particular Dr Max Hernandez, Dr Robert L. Tyson and Mrs Anne-Marie Sandler read drafts at various stages and helped us with their comments. Financial support was provided by the Bethlem Royal Hospital and the Maudsley Hospital Research Fund as well as the Foundation for Research in Psychoanalysis, Los Angeles. We valued in particular the personal interest shown by Mrs Lita Hazen and Dr Ralph R. Greenson of the latter foundation. We gratefully acknowledge the permission given to us by Sigmund Freud Copyrights Ltd, The Institute of Psycho-Analysis, Mrs Alix Strachey and The Hogarth Press Ltd, for permission to quote from the Standard Edition of the *Complete Psychological Works of Sigmund Freud*, revised and edited by James Strachey.

London,
March, 1971

Contents

Chapter 1

Introduction

This book is about the basic psychoanalytic clinical concepts. Many concepts which have developed within psychoanalysis, and in particular those dealt with in this book, have been extended for use within other frames of reference than psychoanalysis, and in very different settings. If psychoanalytic concepts are useful then such extension should be possible and of value, but it seems inevitable that in the process of extension changes in meaning will occur. It is one of the purposes of this book to examine a number of fundamental concepts from this point of view, and the first two chapters will serve to introduce the discussion of specific terms. The philosophical implications of change of meaning when concepts are transferred from their original context has been discussed by a number of writers (e.g. Schon, 1963; Kaplan, 1964), and in this connection psychoanalytic theory presents special problems of its own. It is often regarded as being a completely integrated and consistent system of thought, but this is far from being the case. Psychoanalytic concepts are not all well defined, and changes in their meaning have occurred as psychoanalysis has developed and its theories have changed. We hope to show some of these changes in the pages that follow. Moreover, the same term has been used with different meanings even at the same point in the development of psychoanalysis. A prime example of this is the multiple meaning of such terms as *ego* (Hartmann, 1956), or of *identification* and *introjection* (Sandler, 1960b). It will be seen how strikingly the problems of multiple meaning enter into the particular concepts considered in this book. We find a situation within psychoanalysis at the present time in which the meaning of a concept is only fully discernible from an examination of the

11

context in which it is used. The situation is complicated still further by the fact that different schools of psychodynamic thought have inherited (and then modified for their own use) much of the same basic terminology.*

The overall purpose of the present work can be regarded as an attempt to facilitate communication, not only within the realm of clinical psychoanalysis itself, but also where situations other than the classical psychoanalytic treatment situation (e.g. psychotherapy and some forms of casework) need to be conceptualized in appropriate psychodynamic terms (cf. Sandler, 1969). This need is all the greater in view of the increasing emphasis being placed on training in psychotherapy as part of general psychiatric education (Hill, 1969).

In this context it is worth remembering that psychoanalysis refers not only to a specific treatment method but also to a body of theory which aspires to be a general psychology. Some of its concepts can be regarded as predominantly technical or clinical and do not form part of the general psychological model of psychoanalysis. Clinical concepts of this sort include, for example, that of *resistance*, which refers to a set of clinical phenomena, but which can be seen, in its turn, as a specific manifestation of the operation of the psychological mechanisms of defence (which are part of general psychoanalytic psychology and regarded as existing in 'normal' as well as in disturbed persons). The distinction between clinical psychoanalytic concepts and psychological ones (Freud used the term 'metapsychological') is worth bearing in mind.

We have the situation in which not only the more purely psychological but also the clinical concepts of psychoanalysis have been extended outside the psychoanalytic consulting room. It would appear that these may be capable of application in some degree to any therapeutic situation, but such application may necessitate some degree of re-evaluation and possible redefinition of the concepts used. Thus, if we refer to resistance again, it has been defined in psychoanalysis as resistance to free association, but there is no doubt that essentially the same phenomenon may show itself even in pharmacotherapy in the form of a patient's failure to take helpful medication. While this may reflect a process of

* E.g. the meanings given to *ego*, *self* and *libido* in Jungian psychology are strikingly different from their usages in the Freudian literature.

resistance similar to that seen by the psychoanalyst, its definition in terms of free association cannot be sustained. All psychiatrists and social caseworkers are familiar with the phenomenon of resistance even though forms of communication other than free association are involved.

The wish to give a precise definition of a concept, particularly a clinical one, cannot be entirely fulfilled if the concept is to be used in a variety of clinical situations. The search for precise definitions has led to difficulties and inconsistencies in the various presentations of psychoanalytic concepts in the increasingly available psychoanalytic glossaries and dictionaries (e.g. Laplanche and Pontalis, 1967; Moore and Fine, 1967; Eidelberg, 1968; Rycroft, 1968). It is clear from both the virtues and shortcomings of all these dictionaries that a historical approach is a *sine qua non* for the understanding of any psychoanalytic concept, for its meaning is embedded in the context in which it has been used. For these reasons, therefore, we will take the historical approach.

Psychoanalysis developed to a very large extent in and through the work of Freud, but during the course of its evolution Freud himself modified his formulations many times, revising concepts and adding new dimensions to technical procedures. This is also true of psychoanalysis after Freud. Thus when one talks of one or other aspect of psychoanalysis one has to stamp it with a date, and it is convenient to divide the history of psychoanalysis into a number of phases (after Rapaport, 1959), beginning with Freud's early work.

After qualifying in medicine in Vienna in 1881, and working for a while as a physiologist in Meynert's laboratory, Freud journeyed to France to study with the eminent neurologist Charcot. There he was impressed by the parallel which Charcot drew between the phenomenon of mental dissociation which could be induced by hypnosis and the dissociation between a conscious and an unconscious part of the mind which appeared to occur in patients with gross hysterical symptoms. This dissociation was regarded by Charcot, and by other French psychiatrists, notably Janet, as being due to some acquired or inherited fault in the nervous system, so that the mind could not be held together in one piece, so to speak. On returning to Vienna, Freud began his collaboration with Josef Breuer, a physician who, some years previously, had found that a patient suffering from hysterical symptoms

13

experienced relief if allowed to talk freely under hypnosis. During and following his work with Breuer, Freud became convinced that the process of dissociation into conscious and unconscious regions of the mind was not specific to the psychoneuroses, but occurred in everyone. The appearance of neurotic symptoms was regarded as being due to the breakthrough of pent-up unconscious forces which could not find an adequate expression in some other way. He now saw this dissociation as *active*, as a process of defence whereby consciousness was protected from being overwhelmed by feelings and memories which were unpleasant or threatening. This belief in a process of active dissociation is one which has remained, in one form or another, as a central viewpoint in psychoanalytic writings, although at different times Freud and others have emphasized different aspects of the content of the dissociated and unconscious part of the mind. Initially, particularly during the course of his early work with Breuer, the unconscious content which was being defended against was regarded as consisting of emotionally-charged memories of a real traumatic event. In the book which Freud published jointly with Breuer – the well-known *Studies on Hysteria* (1895) – *real* traumatic events were thought to lie behind the symptoms of the neurotic patient. Such traumatic experiences were postulated as having given rise to a 'charge of affect'. This, together with the memories of the traumatic event, was actively dissociated from consciousness, and could find expression by being converted into symptoms. Based on this view, treatment consisted of a variety of attempts to force the forgotten memories into consciousness, simultaneously bringing about a discharge of affect in the form of catharsis or abreaction.

The *first phase* of psychoanalysis can be taken to include Freud's work with Breuer, and lasted till 1897, when Freud discovered that many of the 'memories' of traumatic experiences, especially seductions, given to him by his hysterical patients were not in fact memories of real events at all, but rather accounts of fantasies (Freud, 1887–1902).

The *second phase* can be regarded as having lasted from the point at which Freud rejected the trauma theory of neurosis to the early 1920's, when he introduced the so-called structural model of psychoanalysis (Freud, 1923). The second phase reflected a change from the early emphasis on external events (the traumatic situation) to an emphasis on unconscious inner wishes, promptings and drives, and to the way in which these impulses manifested themselves on the surface. At this time the unconscious wishes came to be seen as largely sexual in nature. It was the phase in which attention was shifted predominantly to what came from within, to the way in which childhood reactions were repeated over and over again in the present and to the study of what we might call the translation by the analyst of what was consciously brought by the patient into its unconscious meaning. Indeed, the aim of psychoanalysis was seen by Freud as being 'to make what is unconscious conscious'. In this phase, as we might expect when we consider the inevitable to and fro of theory development, there was a radical swing from the consideration of the person's relation to external reality to the study of his relation to his unconscious wishes and impulses. Most of the clinical concepts which we consider in detail in this book, as we shall see, had their original elaborations in the second phase of psychoanalysis.

In 1900 Freud published *The Interpretation of Dreams*. His study of dreams provided an example of the way in which unconscious wishes were thought to find their way to the surface. The urge for direct expression of these wishes created a situation of *conflict* with the individual's assessment of reality and with his ideals. This conflict, between instinctual forces on the one hand, and repressive or defensive forces which were called into play on the other, resulted in the construction of compromise-formations which represented attempts at obtaining fulfilment of the unconscious wishes in disguised form. Thus the *manifest dream content* could be considered to be a 'censored', or disguised fulfilment of an unconscious wish. Similarly the free associations of the patient in analysis were also regarded as disguised derivatives of unconscious wishes.

In the second phase, as in the first, Freud assumed that there was a part of the mind – the 'mental apparatus' – which was conscious, and a further, substantial unconscious part. In this connection, Freud distinguished between two sorts of unconsciousness. One, represented by a 'system' – the *Unconscious* – contained instinctual drives and wishes which, if they were to be allowed to emerge into consciousness would constitute a danger, a threat, and would give rise to anxiety or other unpleasant feelings. The strivings in the Unconscious were seen as being constantly pro-

15

pelled towards discharge, but could only be allowed expression in a distorted or censored form. The other sort of unconsciousness was that attributed to the *Preconscious* system, and contained knowledge and thoughts which were outside consciousness but not held back by the counterforces of repression, as were contents relegated to the Unconscious. Preconscious mental content could enter into consciousness at the appropriate time, and could be utilized by the individual not only for rational tasks but could also be seized upon by wishes from the Unconscious in their attempts to force a passage through to consciousness. The model of the mental apparatus in the second phase is generally known as the 'topographical' model, and in it the Preconscious system was thought of as lying between the Unconscious and consciousness (the quality of the system *Conscious*).

Freud saw the instinctual drives as 'energies' which could be invested in different mental contents. He made use of the term *libido* for the sexual energy of the instinctual drives, and although aggression was later given a status equal in importance to sexuality, he coined no corresponding term for 'aggressive energy'. The hypothetical drive energy could be invested* in mental content of one sort or another. In the Unconscious these energies were regarded as being freely displaceable from one content to another, and functioned according to the so-called *primary process*. Logical and formal relations between the elements in the Unconscious were regarded as absent, with only simple and primitive rules of association applying, with no awareness of time present. Drives and wishes in the Unconscious functioned according to the 'pleasure-principle', i.e. were regarded as seeking discharge, gratification and relief of painful tension at all costs. The systems Preconscious and Conscious could be considered as being in direct opposition to this. Here logic, reason (*secondary process*) and the knowledge of external reality and of ideals and standards of conduct predominate. In opposition to the Unconscious, the Preconscious and Conscious systems take (or attempt to take) external reality into account, to follow what Freud called the 'reality-principle'. Thus situations of conflict – for example between sexual wishes of a primitive sort which had been repressed into the Unconscious and the person's moral and ethical standards – must inevitably arise, and some

* In English translations of Freud, the German word for 'investment' (*Besetzung*) has been (in our view unfortunately) rendered as 'cathexis'.

16

sort of solution sought which would take the opposing forces into account.

Thus far we have referred to the instinctual drives and instinctual wishes as if they were regarded as existing somewhat in isolation. In Freud's view this was far from being the case, as from early in the child's development the instinctual urges were seen as having become attached to important figures in the child's world – or objects, to use the unfortunately impersonal term which is employed by psychoanalysts to describe these emotionally significant figures. Every unconscious wish was regarded as having an object, and the same object could be the recipient of quite opposing wishes – manifested typically in feelings of both love and hate for the same person. This in itself is a most potent source of mental conflict – the conflict of *ambivalence*. Freud took the view that people, in their later adult relationships to others, repeated (often in a very disguised way) their infantile attachments and conflicts, and that this tendency to repetition was often at the root of a great many of the difficulties which his patients brought.

Among the early conflicts of the child reconstructed through analysis, one constellation was thought to be universal, the Oedipus complex, in which the child, at about the age of four or five, has to deal with a conflict in regard to his wishes and object-relationships of the most intense sort. Essentially it is regarded as the wish of the little boy to have intercourse with his mother, to possess her completely and to get rid of father in some way, not the most uncommon way being the wish to have him die. These wishes were seen by Freud as being in conflict with the little boy's love for his father and also his fear of rejection or bodily damage at his hands – in particular the fear of father's retaliatory damage to his genitals, so-called castration anxiety. The picture in regard to the little girl is somewhat similar, the roles of the parents being reversed, although in *both* boys and girls the two opposing constellations are thought to exist. Thus we find in the boy a wish to be possessed by the father and to be rid of mother, a consequence of innate bisexuality in everyone, male or female.

These views on mental functioning and infantile sexuality were the product of the second phase, and represented a period of intense study of the vicissitudes of unconscious instinctual drives, particularly sexual drives (1905a) and their derivatives. It has been described here at some length because of its importance for the more detailed consideration of the clinical concepts discussed in the chapters which follow. In the context of the psychological model of the second phase these concepts can be regarded as relatively simple and straightforward. However, as we shall show, developments in Freud's own thinking caused complications to appear.

The *third phase* can be dated from 1923, when a decisive change occurred in Freud's conceptualization of mental functioning. Deeply impressed by the operation in his patients in what he could only conceive of as an unconscious sense of guilt, and because of a number of inconsistencies and contradictions which were emerging in the detailed application of the 'topographical' division of the mental apparatus into the systems Unconscious, Preconscious and Conscious, he put forward a revised theoretical model. Perhaps it would be more appropriate to say that he introduced a further point of view, for his new formulations were not entirely to replace the older but rather to exist alongside them. It was such a situation which we had in mind when we referred earlier to the fact that we do not have a consistent, coherent and fully integrated theoretical model in psychoanalysis. Thus in 1923, for the reasons we have alluded to, Freud introduced, in *The Ego and the Id*, what has been called the 'structural' model – the three-fold division of the mental apparatus into what he referred to as id, ego and superego.

The *id* was seen as corresponding roughly to much of what had been encompassed by the concept of the Unconscious in the past. It can be regarded as that area of the mind containing the primitive instinctual drives, with all their hereditary and constitutional elements. It is dominated by the pleasure principle, and functions according to the primary process. During maturation and development, and as a consequence of the interaction with the external world, a portion of the id undergoes modification to become the *ego*. The primary function of this latter agency was seen as the task of self-preservation and the acquisition of means whereby a simultaneous adaptation to the pressures of the id and the demands of reality can be brought about. It gains the function of delaying instinctual discharge, or of controlling it by means of a variety of mechanisms, including the mechanisms of defence. The third agency, the *superego*, was seen as developing as a sort of internal precipitate or residue of the child's early conflicts and identifications, particularly in relation to his parents or other figures of authority. It is the vehicle of the conscience, including that part of the conscience which is regarded as unconscious, for a large part of the superego, as well as the ego, and all of the id, was seen as functioning outside consciousness.

It is worth mentioning that in this 'structural' theory there is again a change of emphasis from that which dominated the previous phase. The ego's role was seen to be that of a mediator, a problem-solver, having at each and every moment to meet the demands arising from the id, from the superego and from the external world. In order to resolve these often conflicting demands the ego has at times to create the most complicated compromises, and in the last resort these compromises may result in the symptoms which, although painful and distressing to the individual who experiences them, represent the best possible adaptation that he can, in the particular circumstances, bring about. Such compromises are regarded as entering into the formation of character and personality, into choice of career and love-objects and into all those things which go into making any one person a unique individual.

This particular phase in the development of psychoanalysis lasted till Freud's death in 1939. This is a rather arbitrary dating, for what we can refer to as the *fourth phase* represents the contributions of psychoanalysts other than Freud. These began to make important additions to theory and practice from the time that colleagues first came to be associated with Freud in his work and identified themselves with his point of view.

An important line of development in the fourth phase of psycho-analytic theory, although it was evident in Freud's work, was given a strong impetus by the publication in 1936 of Anna Freud's *The Ego and the Mechanisms of Defence* and in 1939 of Heinz Hartmann's *Ego Psychology and the Problem of Adaptation*. Anna Freud drew attention to the role of defence mechanisms in normal mental functioning, and introduced the concept of defence against dangers arising from the external world as well as against those linked with internal instinctual impulses. Hartmann placed special emphasis on the innate development of what he called the conflict-free sphere of the ego. Whereas Freud had orientated himself constantly towards clinical phenomena, and to the way in which special skills and capacities can develop in the individual as means of resolving conflict, Hartmann maintained that there are many areas of normal functioning which have a primary course of development of their own. What is called 'ego psychology' represents the special interests of many psychoanalysts who have placed normal as well as abnormal ego functioning at the centre of their attention. However, the relevant contributions of psychoanalysts other than Freud will be discussed throughout this book where appropriate, and there is no need to mention them specifically here. It is necessary to point out, however, that much of current psychoanalytic thinking, particularly that part related to the clinical situation, is still firmly rooted in the second phase of psychoanalysis. We find the situation in which psychoanalysts, in describing their patients, make use of topographical (i.e. second phase) concepts alongside those of the structural theory of the third phase, although heroic efforts have been made by certain psychoanalysts (e.g. Arlow and Brenner, 1964) to write current psychoanalytic theory entirely in terms of the concepts of the structural theory.

Chapter 2

The Clinical Situation

The clinical concepts used to describe, explain and understand the psychoanalytic treatment process have arisen at different points in the history of psychoanalysis. Terms which derived their original meaning in the context of one phase have been carried over into later phases, with the sort of repercussions which we have alluded to earlier and shall discuss later. In this chapter we shall try to describe the development of the psychoanalytic treatment setting in relation to the different phases of psychoanalysis (see Chap. 1).

The first phase (which was essentially pre-psychoanalytic) lasted until 1897, and was principally characterized by the application of the hypnotic method to hysterical patients. With the inclusion of patients suffering from other disturbances (e.g. obsessional disorders) Freud saw his methods as being applicable to the 'neuro-psychoses' (which would now be called the neuroses). The treatment setting in the first phase was essentially that in use at the time for inducing hypnosis in the consulting room (i.e. in privacy, as opposed to the public demonstrations of such workers as Charcot). The situation was one in which the patient lay on a couch and the therapist, sitting behind the patient, induced a state of hypnosis. Later Freud tried to encourage the recall of forgotten events without hypnosis by a variety of methods. One of these was to apply pressure with his hand to the patient's forehead with the suggestion that this would bring thoughts to mind, as described in the case of Frau P. J. (1887–1902). While such techniques were later to be replaced by 'free association' on the part of the patient, the structure of the treatment situation of the first phase persisted. As Freud put it (1925):

'My patients, I reflected, must in fact "know" all the things which had hitherto only been made accessible to them in hypnosis; and assurances and encouragement on my part . . . . would, I thought, have the power of forcing the forgotten facts and connections into consciousness. No doubt this seemed a more laborious process than putting the patients into hypnosis, but it might prove highly instructive. So I abandoned hypnosis, only retaining my practice of requiring the patient to lie upon a sofa while I sat behind him, seeing him, but not seen myself.'

In Chapter 1 we have described Freud's change in 1897 from the traumatogenic theory of neurosis to one in which the role of conflict over the expression of unconscious instinctual wishes was seen to be of paramount importance. This change of view coincided, more or less, with the technical emphasis on unravelling the meaning of the patient's conscious productions, in particular his dreams which, in the early years of the second phase, were regarded as being the most important part of the patient's material.* Much of Freud's analytic work was initially directed towards the painstaking analysis of the dream, the analyst being assisted by the patient's associations to the various parts of the remembered dream. Dream analysis provided the basis for Freud's understanding of mental processes in general, although as the second phase progressed, the understanding of the unconscious meaning of the patient's productions was extended to his free associations in general, and analysis of transference, especially of transference resistances, came to play a major role in psychoanalytic technique. During the second phase, which lasted until 1923, the basic psychoanalytic treatment setting, and the clinical concepts related to it, were developed. Although major theoretical changes occurred during the third and fourth phases of psychoanalysis, the 'classical' psychoanalytic treatment situation has remained essentially that of the second phase. By the time Freud came to write the 'technical' papers on psychoanalysis (1911b, 1912a, 1912b, 1913a, 1914a, 1915a) the technique had been formalized. It is worth noting however, that, at that time, the patient was expected to attend six days a week, for sessions of an hour each.

The 'basic model of psychoanalysis' (Eissler, 1953) can be

* Dreams are still regarded as the most important source of material by some psychoanalysts, and still have a special significance for all analysts.

described as follows. The patient is, as a rule, in possession of relatively few personal facts about the psychoanalyst. The analyst attempts to maintain this area of relative ignorance on the patient's part, but encourages him to talk as freely as possible about his thoughts as they come into his mind during the daily sessions. In Great Britain, as in many other countries, this daily session is of fifty minutes' duration, five times a week. The psychoanalyst's contributions will normally tend to be limited to questions to elucidate the material and to *interpretations, confrontations* and *reconstructions* (see Chap. 10) which represent the major therapeutic interventions. In the course of his associations the patient will begin to evade certain topics and to show *resistance* (see Chap. 7) to expressing certain thoughts and to the psychoanalytic procedure. The psychoanalyst expects that the material produced by the patient will, sooner or later, contain overt or covert references to thoughts and feelings about the psychoanalyst which will have the quality of distortion of reality which is referred to as *transference* (see Chaps. 4 and 5). These distortions are the result of the modification of the patient's present perceptions and thoughts by the addition of specific components derived from past wishes, experiences and relationships. A distinction is often made between such transference phenomena and the working relationship which develops between patient and psychoanalyst based, among other things, on the patient's wish to recover and to co-operate in treatment. The *treatment alliance* (see Chap. 3) is regarded as including, as an essential part, the patient's motivation for continuing in analysis in the face of his resistances. At times the patient will not bring emergent past and present feelings verbally but rather in the form of behaviour and acts which may also be expressed in a displaced form outside the consulting room. This is often referred to as an aspect of *acting out* (see Chap. 9).

The demands of the psychoanalytic procedure on the analyst naturally include his conscious attempts to understand the patient's material in order to make his interventions. In addition to this he is faced with the necessity to scan his reactions to the patient in an attempt to determine his own blocks in appreciating the meaning of the patient's communications. Such self-scanning also enables him to obtain, through his appreciation of his own emotional responses to the patient, further insight into what is going on in the patient. These aspects of the analyst's reactions are conceptualized as *counter-transference* (see Chap. 6). If the patient is able to gain and to retain an understanding of links between his conscious and unconscious tendencies, and between the present and the past, he is said to have acquired a degree of *insight* (see Chap. 10).

Interpretations given by the analyst, even if they seem to increase the patient's insight, are not always immediately effective in producing a significant change in the patient. A period of time has to be allowed for *working through* (see Chap. 11) during which time the ramifications both of interpretations and the material encompassed by them are explored and extended.

At times when the patient appears to have made significant progress he may have what appears to be a paradoxical relapse. This may be a manifestation of a *negative therapeutic reaction* (see Chap. 8), usually attributed to the workings of an unconscious sense of guilt (Freud, 1923), related to the significance to the patient of a perceived improvement.

It is obvious that the 'model situation' as described here does not apply to every psychoanalytic treatment, and special alterations of the technical procedure have to be introduced. These have been referred to as 'parameters of technique' (Eissler, 1953), but the introduction of such 'parameters' is seen, from the point of view of the basic model of psychoanalysis, as a temporary expedient. In this respect, the methods of psychoanalysis have been contrasted with those other forms of psychotherapy in which the so-called 'parameters' have been extensively employed. Adaptations of psychoanalytic technique to make it suitable for special classes of disturbances have been increasingly prominent during the fourth phase of psychoanalysis.

The bald and simplified account given in the first two chapters is intended to serve as an introduction to the more detailed examination of some of the clinical psychoanalytic concepts which have been referred to. In the chapters which follow we discuss the historical vicissitudes of each concept within the clinical framework of psychoanalysis. We also examine the multiplicities and ambiguities of meanings within that framework, and explore the degree to which such concepts are available for application in situations other than that of classical psychoanalytic treatment.

24

Clinical Regression

A feature of the psychoanalytic process which deserves special mention is the occurrence of the phenomenon of regression. While the term 'regression' has been used in a number of senses in psychoanalytic theory, we are concerned in this book with one specific meaning of the term, i.e. the emergence of past, often infantile, trends where such trends are thought to represent the reappearance of modes of functioning which had been abandoned or modified. Regression of this sort appears as a characteristic part of the psychoanalytic process, but the same phenomena are visible outside analysis. We need only quote the way in which a toddler can relinquish bowel control in the period of stress following the birth of a sibling, or the way in which a child (or adult) may become clinging and demanding when hospitalized. Such regressions, which may affect any part of personality functioning, may be temporary or more permanent, slight or severe. Regressions of this sort are to be expected at critical phases in the individual's development and, unless unusually prolonged or severe, may be regarded as normal (A. Freud, 1965).

In psychoanalytic treatment one of the functions of the setting is to permit, or to facilitate regression. Regressive trends are seen most clearly in analysis as transference phenomena develop, in the re-emergence of childhood wishes, feelings, modes of relating, fantasies and behaviour towards the person of the analyst. However, as well as being an essential vehicle whereby important data are brought from the past in a convincing and meaningful way, regression may at times also have a more obstructive and damaging aspect. This is particularly so when it becomes so intense or prolonged that the patient is unable to regain that capacity for self-observation which is a necessary part of the treatment alliance (see Chap. 3).

For example, it is quite a common experience in the course of an analysis that the patient will become, at some stage, increasingly demanding of love, affection and tokens of esteem from the analyst. The way in which this shows itself can be an important source of understanding in regard to the early relationship between the patient and, for instance, a mother who was experienced as depriving or withdrawn. Such information may constitute essential material for understanding the patient's current difficulties and problems. However, if such demandingness becomes the main point of the patient's communications to the analyst, and the analyst is unable to reverse this trend through appropriate interpretations or other interventions, the capacity to pursue the analytic work may be impaired or even, in certain cases, lost. This is evident in certain special forms of transference (see Chap. 5).

A number of authors have pointed out the importance of the ability to regress inside and outside the psychoanalytic situation. For example, Kris (1952) has discussed the importance of the capacity for controlled and temporary regression in the realm of artistic creativity. Winnicott (1954) and Balint (1934, 1965, 1968) have stressed the importance of the patient's regression as a means of obtaining access to material which would not otherwise be available. Balint has called this 'regression in the service of progression'. It appears to be likely that different psychoanalysts vary in the degree to which they (consciously or unconsciously) encourage regressive trends in their patients.

Chapter 3

The Treatment Alliance

Psychiatry and other disciplines have been paying increasing attention in recent years to the relationship between patient and doctor, and psychoanalytic concepts have been applied in order to formulate various aspects of this relationship. One of those most commonly taken from its original context and applied outside it is that of *transference*, which is now often loosely used in a variety of senses. It is even used as a synonym for 'relationship' in general. We will discuss the concept of transference in more detail in Chapters 4 and 5.

A distinction has always been made within clinical psycho-analysis between 'transference proper' and another aspect of the patient's relation to the doctor which has been referred to in recent years as the 'therapeutic alliance', 'working alliance' or 'treatment alliance' (Zetzel, 1956; Loewald, 1960; Stone, 1961, 1967; Gitelson, 1962; Tarachow, 1963; Greenson, 1965a, 1967; Fried-man, 1969). The concept has been used in connection with the psychoanalytic treatment situation to describe aspects of what is familiar to many as the 'therapeutic contract' (Menninger, 1958) between the patient and his doctor. This is essentially what has been defined as 'the non-neurotic, rational, reasonable rapport which the patient has with his analyst and which enables him to work purposefully in the analytic situation' (Greenson and Wexler, 1969). This notion, as it has developed, has come to cover far more than the patient's conscious wish to get better, a point to which we will return later. As far as the psychoanalytic situation is concerned, it has been maintained that the recognition of the difference between 'treatment alliance' and other aspects of the

27

patient-analyst interaction (such as transference) leads to an increased understanding of the processes which occur in that situation and, in particular, of those which enter into therapeutic failure. For psychoanalysis and other methods of treatment as well, the assessment of the capacity to develop a treatment alliance is relevant at the stage at which a decision has to be made with regard to the appropriate form of treatment.

It is the purpose of this chapter to examine the treatment alliance concept as it has developed within psychoanalysis, and to consider its applicability outside the treatment situation.

The notion of a treatment alliance had its origin within psychoanalysis in Freud's writings on technique, although it was never designated by Freud as a distinctive concept. It was originally encompassed within the general concept of transference which at that time he divided into transference of positive feelings on the one hand and negative transferences on the other (Freud, 1912a). Positive transferences were further seen as divisible into transference of friendly or affectionate feelings (of which the patient was aware) and transferences which represented the return, possibly in a distorted form, of childhood erotic relationships. The latter were not normally remembered but rather re-experienced by the patient towards the person of the analyst (see Chaps. 4, 5 and 9). Such positive transferences, together with negative transferences, could develop into resistance to treatment (see Chap. 7). The friendly and affectionate component of the positive transference was described as representing 'the vehicle of success in psychoanalysis, exactly as it is in other methods of treatment'.

In a subsequent paper (Freud, 1913a) reference was made to the need to establish 'an effective transference' before the full work of psychoanalysis could begin. Freud maintained that it was necessary to wait 'until an effective transference has been established in the patient, a proper *rapport* with him. It remains the first aim of treatment to attach him to it and to the person of the doctor.' The essential distinction made by Freud at this time was between the patient's capacity to establish a friendly rapport and attachment to the doctor on the one hand, and the emergence, within the framework of the treatment, of revived feelings and attitudes which could become an obstacle to therapeutic progress. The fact that Freud used the term 'transference' for both these aspects

28

of the relationship has been a source of confusion in subsequent literature and has contributed to the persisting use of the term 'positive transference' to designate aspects of what we refer to here as the treatment alliance.*

The concept of a treatment alliance is implied in two papers by Richard Sterba (1934, 1940), who emphasized the need for the psychoanalyst to bring about a separation within the patient of those elements which are focused on reality from those which are not. The reality-focused elements allow the patient to identify with the aims of the therapist, a process which Sterba regarded as an essential condition for successful psychoanalytic treatment. This is consistent with a reference by Freud (1933) to the necessity, in successful treatment, for the patient to utilize his capacity to observe himself as if he were another person. In this context, Fenichel (1941) has written of a 'reasonable' aspect of the patient, and of what he calls a 'rational transference'. In tracing this concept through the psychoanalytic literature, it has become evident that the 'friendly transference', 'effective transference', 'reality-focused elements', 'rational transference' and self-observing and self-critical capacities are often treated as if they were equivalent, whereas they can more usefully be seen as separate elements which can be brought under the general heading of treatment alliance.

Following an important paper by Elizabeth Zetzel (1956), psychoanalytic writers have been increasingly concerned with differentiating the treatment alliance from transference 'proper'. A trend in more recent publications, reflected in the work of

---

* We can probably link the crystallization of a concept of treatment alliance as something other than a special aspect of transference (i.e. the 'friendly' transference) with the development of what has come to be known as 'ego psychology'. This aspect of psychoanalytic thinking developed after the formulation of the 'structural' model of the mental apparatus (Freud, 1923, 1926a), in which the concept of the ego, as an organized part of the personality having to cope with the outside world and the conscience (*superego*), as well as with the instinctual drives (*id*), was elaborated. Subsequent psychoanalytic writers (e.g. Anna Freud, 1965; Hartmann, 1939, 1964) have developed the notion of ego functions and attributes which are relatively independent of the drives ('autonomous ego functions'). Much of what has been written about the treatment alliance concept in its various forms implies that it makes use of such 'autonomous' functions and attitudes.

Greenson (1965a, 1967) and Greenson and Wexler (1969), is to regard the core of the treatment alliance as being anchored in the 'real' or 'non-transference' relationship which the patient establishes with his doctor.

There appears to be a strong case for distinguishing the concept of the treatment alliance from other aspects of the patient's relationship to his doctor, which are not sufficient in themselves to form a successful basis for psychoanalytic treatment. These include the revival of loving or sexual feelings originally directed towards an important figure of the patient's past, showing themselves in extreme forms by the patient falling in love with the therapist. They also include idealization of the therapist in which he is seen as perfect or supremely capable – an idealization which can cover underlying hostile feelings and which may break down (often quite dramatically) if the patient feels disappointed or if hostile feelings become too strong. The ability to develop a treatment alliance is thought to draw on qualities which have become a relatively stable part of the individual. While it is true that these qualities may be related, in their development, to successful aspects of the child's early relationships, they appear to be, to an important degree, independent of those feelings and attitudes which can be conceptualized as 'transference'. Thus the treatment alliance can be regarded as

'being based on the patient's conscious or unconscious wish to co-operate, and his readiness to accept the therapist's aid in overcoming internal difficulties. This is not the same as attending treatment simply on the basis of getting pleasure or some other form of gratification. In the treatment alliance there is an *acceptance* of the need to deal with internal problems, and to do analytic work in the face of internal or (particularly with children) external (e.g. family) resistance' (Sandler *et al*, 1969).

It seems clear that this concept must also draw upon what Erikson has called 'basic trust' (1950), an attitude to people and the world in general which is based on the infant's experiences of security in the first months of life. The absence of the quality of 'basic trust' is thought to account for the absence of a fully-functioning treatment alliance in certain psychotics and in others who have experienced severe emotional deprivation as children.

As Erikson has put it (1950): 'In psychopathology the absence of basic trust can best be studied in infantile schizophrenia,* while weakness of such trust is apparent in adult personalities of schizoid and depressive character. The re-establishment of a state of trust has been found to be the basic requirement for therapy in these cases.'

As we have said, the treatment alliance should not be equated with the patient's wish to get better. While this wish certainly contributes to the treatment alliance, it may also carry with it unreal and even magical expectations from treatment – unreliable allies in the therapeutic task. The unreliability of the wish for recovery as the sole basis of the treatment alliance is emphasized in the psychoanalytic literature in descriptions of those cases who break off treatment as soon as there is a degree of symptomatic relief, and who lose any desire to explore the factors leading to their illness once the symptoms have lessened or disappeared. Recovery may also represent a 'flight into health' and, if the treatment alliance in such cases is based only on the wish for relief of symptoms, no adequate basis for the continuation of psychoanalytic treatment remains, even though the patient may know from his own history that his relief from suffering may be only temporary. It would appear that most of the elements mentioned by the psychoanalytic writers on the topic (the capacity to regard oneself as one might regard another, the capacity to tolerate a certain amount of frustration, the existence of a degree of 'basic trust', identification with the aims of treatment, etc.) are, to some degree, essential.

It may be difficult, especially at the beginning of treatment, to distinguish the patient's capacity for establishing and maintaining a treatment alliance from positive feelings towards the therapist and towards treatment which stem from other sources. Apparent regard or even affection for the therapist and initial willingness to attend do not necessarily indicate that the patient is ready to continue to work in therapy. This is highlighted in those cases where the patient asks for help in order to appease a relative or

---

* The meaning of the term 'infantile schizophrenia' as used by Erikson is not clear. We would probably refer today to infantile psychosis or autism, and to the severe personality problems of the multiply-deprived child.

31

even his general practitioner, and in some people undergoing psychoanalysis as a required part of a psychoanalytic training course (Gitelson, 1954). In cases where no adequate treatment alliance exists, it appears to be essential to determine (a) whether the patient has the capacity for forming such an alliance, and (b) whether he can develop sufficient appropriate motivation to develop a treatment alliance of sufficient degree to enable him to weather the stresses and strains of treatment.

A patient may remain in treatment because it gratifies concealed wishes (e.g. for dependence, for attention and love, and even for masochistic suffering). A consequence of this is that the patient may continue in psychoanalytic treatment for many years, showing no inclination to leave, yet showing no significant improvement. However, it is equally possible that a useful treatment alliance may exist when the patient is initially hostile. It should be noted that there are some people who have strong paranoid trends in their personality, who are supremely 'untrusting', and who are still able to establish some sort of treatment alliance with the therapist. In some way they appear to recognize their need for help, and make an 'exception' of the therapist.

It should be pointed out that some psychoanalytic writers do not accept the necessity of a treatment alliance as a prerequisite for psychoanalytic treatment, and would tend to apply the same technique to all cases. An example of this is the technique developed by Melanie Klein and her followers (Segal, 1964; Meltzer, 1967) in which all communications by and behaviour of the patient in treatment tend to be conceptualized and interpreted as transference of postulated infantile attitudes and feelings. However, W. Bion, a member of the Kleinian school, has referred to 'task-relatedness' in groups (1961), and this may be taken to imply some aspect of what we have been discussing under the heading of 'treatment alliance'. The Kleinian approach has been criticized as being an inadequate and even impoverished conceptualization (e.g. by Glover, 1945; Joffe, 1969) although its simplicity and apparent 'depth' of approach appear to contribute to its appeal as a system of therapy.

Treatment can, of course, be begun without a strong treatment alliance, although some form of therapeutic 'contract' is usually necessary at the outset of treatment. A treatment alliance may, and ideally should, develop during the course of treatment. It also appears to be a major part of the work of the psychoanalyst to assist the development of a treatment alliance. Such assistance can take the form of providing a constant and regular setting for the patient's communications (see Chap. 2). It also includes the interpretation by the analyst to the patient of the patient's resistances to the development of an adequate treatment alliance. An example of the latter would be the analyst's interpretation of how a patient, because of his fear of passive submission, does not allow himself to co-operate fully in the analytic work. Although this resistance may have many sources, it manifests itself, in effect, as a resistance to the treatment alliance, even though, strictly speaking, we could also see it as a resistance to, say, a developing homosexual transference (see Chaps. 4, 5 and 7). A further example of a resistance to the development of an adequate treatment alliance would be the case of a patient who is very afraid of the invitation to regression posed by the analytic situation. While most patients can tolerate, to some degree, their regressive tendencies in the analytic situation, some people are afraid that if they 'let go' they would become completely infantilized, and would lose control over their thoughts and actions. Interpretation of the patient's anxiety may help him to deal with it, and to develop an appropriate treatment alliance.

It follows from what has been said that the treatment alliance should not be regarded as a constant throughout psychoanalytic treatment. It is frequently diminished by the patient's resistances, and augmented by the development of positive feelings. The treatment alliance may be completely disrupted by gross regressive manifestations during treatment (Dickes, 1967). It may also diminish or even disappear if an 'erotized' transference develops (see Chap. 5).

The assessment of a patient's *capacity* to form a treatment alliance is obviously important. Thus most psychoanalysts would not normally take a patient who is grossly psychotic into analysis. The implication here is that the patient does not, at the time, possess the capacity to work analytically and constructively with the therapist. However, treatment may be directed towards the development of this ability.*

* In the past analysts often made use of a 'trial period' of analysis after which a joint decision about continuation could be made. This decision

Occasionally, irrational motives may foster the development of a treatment alliance. An example might be a patient who has very strong sibling rivalry, and works hard at his analysis in order to be more successful than a rival colleague, also in analysis. Here the patient's rivalry, while constituting analytic material to be understood, may for a while help the progress of the analytic work.

The concept of the treatment alliance appears to be readily capable of being extended outside psychoanalysis without substantial modification, although it is true that different clinical 'contracts' (to use Menninger's term) exist in different clinical situations. A treatment alliance would not be required in the emergency treatment of an unconscious patient. At the other extreme, it would seem to be essential for the success of a prolonged course of rehabilitation. In many treatment situations it may be worthwhile to extend the concept to include the capacities and attitudes of the patient's family or of other environmental agencies. In the same way as a treatment alliance is necessary between patient and analyst, it appears to be equally necessary in those situations where the patient cannot carry the burden of treatment on his own. This is particularly the case in the treatment of children, where a treatment alliance with the child's parents is absolutely necessary. It is also necessary in the case of the outpatient treatment of psychotic patients to have such an 'extended' treatment alliance. This is the case no matter what the form of treatment is, as the co-operation of the patient's family may be necessary in order to ensure that he attends at all. In such situations the concept of the treatment alliance becomes more or less synonymous with that of 'co-operativeness'.

The assessment of the capacity for treatment alliance has not yet been the subject of systematic study, although much has been written by psychoanalysts on the topic, and on the related prob-

would be based, in part, on what would nowadays be known as the patient's capacity for a treatment alliance as revealed during the trial period. Similarly, Anna Freud (1928) advocated an 'introductory phase' in child analysis, during which the child was introduced to the idea of treatment and established a bond with the analyst. The recommendation of a pre-analytic introductory phase was later dropped. Hoffer (*Personal communication to J. S.*) has spoken of 'seducing the patient into treatment'.

lems of 'suitability' for psychoanalysis (Tyson and Sandler, 1971). Recent changes in attitudes to mental health, and the growing acceptance of the voluntary principle, must inevitably place increasing weight on the assessment, not only of the patient's insight into his illness, but also of his capacity to form a treatment alliance with his therapist. This applies particularly to psychotic patients and to those patients who have, in the past, been labelled as 'psychopathic' or suffering from 'severe personality disorder' or 'character disorder'. The assessment, during the initial period of doctor-patient interaction, of the patient's capacity for forming a treatment alliance must have diagnostic significance in regard to the severity of the disorder, and prognostic significance where the prognosis is related to the method of treatment. In those cases where psychotherapy is judged to be indicated, the clinical assessment of the patient's ability to tolerate and to co-operate with the therapist in a prolonged, time-consuming and often painful process seems crucial, and the concept of treatment alliance, or of potential for treatment alliance, appears to have value. It is thus useful for the referring physician to come to some decision about the patient's capacity and motivation for developing an enduring treatment alliance which could support the treatment process. But even in situations where there is no question of psychotherapy, the concept of treatment alliance would appear to be useful in considering the nature of the patient's involvement in the treatment situation, and the nature of his relationship with the therapeutic figures in that situation. Certainly in the casework situation, the social worker implicitly assesses the state of the treatment alliance between the client (or the client and his family) and herself. Naturally, the treatment alliance is affected by the requirements of the treatment situation and by the style of work of the particular agency involved. For example, some clients may be able to sustain a relationship with an agency so long as regular appointments are provided, but would not be able to maintain a treatment alliance if the initiative for contact was left to the client. Special and interesting problems arise in the case of persons on probation, who are required to see the probation officer regularly. While compulsory attendance may aid the treatment alliance in some cases, it may produce a 'pseudo-alliance' in others.

The problem of gauging the potential for treatment alliance is,

of course, a familiar problem in psychiatric and physical rehabilitation units, where work and rewards have to be graded to encourage increasing investment and motivation in the programme
provided.

Chapter 4

Transference

In the previous chapter, aspects of the therapist-patient relationship were discussed under the general heading of 'Treatment Alliance'. It was pointed out that the concept included features which have been, at times, referred to as 'transference', and the purpose of the present chapter is to consider some of the further meanings of the latter term. It will be seen from what follows that the concept of *transference* can only be appreciated in terms of its historical development, and that different schools within psycho-analysis tend to emphasize different aspects of the definition of transference. The understanding and analysis of transference phenomena are regarded by psychoanalysts as being at the very centre of their therapeutic technique, and the concept is widely applied outside psychoanalysis in the attempt to understand human relationships in general. A dissection of the various meanings attributed to the word seems necessary in order to consider its current and potential applications.

Freud first made use of the term *transference* when he was reporting on his attempts to elicit verbal associations from his patients (Freud, 1895). The aim of the method of treatment was for the patient to discover, primarily through his associations and emotional responses, the link between his *present* symptoms and feelings on the one hand and his *past* experiences on the other. Freud assumed that the 'dissociation' of the past experiences (and the feelings connected with them) from consciousness was a major factor in the genesis of the neurosis. He noted that changes developed during the course of treatment in the patient's attitude to the physician, and that these changes, involving strong emotional components, could cause an interruption to the process of verbal association, often resulting in substantial obstacles to treatment. He commented (1895) that ' . . . the patient is frightened at finding that she is transferring on to the figure of the physician the distressing ideas which arise from the content of the analysis. This is a frequent, and indeed in some analyses a regular, occurrence.' These feelings were regarded as 'transference', coming about as a consequence of what Freud called a 'false connection' between a person who was the object of earlier (usually sexual) wishes and the doctor. Feelings connected with past wishes (which have been excluded from consciousness) emerge and become experienced in the present as a consequence of the 'false connection'. In this context Freud remarked on the propensity of patients to develop neurotic attachments towards their doctors.

In a paper published some years later (Freud, 1905b), the term 'transference' was once again used in the context of the psychoanalytic treatment situation. Freud put the question:

> 'What are transferences? They are new editions or facsimiles of the impulses and phantasies which are aroused during the progress of the analysis; but they have this peculiarity, which is characteristic for their species, that they replace some earlier person by the person of the physician. To put it another way: a whole series of psychological experiences are revived, not as belonging to the past, but as applying to the person of the physician at the present moment. Some of these transferences have a content which differs from that of their model in no respect whatever except for the substitution. These then – to keep to the same metaphor – are merely new impressions or reprints. Others are more ingeniously constructed; their content has been subjected to a moderating influence . . . by cleverly taking advantage of some real peculiarity in the physician's person or circumstances and attaching themselves to that. These, then, will no longer be new impressions, but revised editions.'

Thus far transference had been seen as a clinical phenomenon which could act as an obstacle or 'resistance' (see Chap. 7) to the analytic work, but a few years later (1909a) Freud remarked that transference was not always an obstacle to analysis but may also play 'a decisive part in bringing conviction not only to the patient but also to the physician'. This is the first mention of transference as a therapeutic agent. It should be noted that Freud consistently distinguished the analysis of transference as a technical measure from the so-called 'transference-cure' in which the patient appears to lose all his symptoms as a consequence of feelings of love for and a wish to please the analyst (1915a).*

Somewhat later Freud pointed out that 'a transference is present in the patient from the beginning of the treatment and for a while is the most powerful motive in its advance' (1916–17). By now it would appear that Freud was using the term to include a number of rather different phenomena, although they all had the quality of being seen as a repetition of past feelings and attitudes in the present. In 1912 Freud had spoken of 'positive' transferences as opposed to 'negative' ones, and had further subdivided positive transferences into those which helped the therapeutic work and those which hindered it. Negative transferences were regarded as the transference of hostile feelings towards the therapist, the extreme form being manifested in paranoia, though in a milder form it could be seen to co-exist with positive transference in all patients. This co-existence enabled the patient to use one aspect of his transference to protect himself against the disturbing emergence of the other. Thus a patient might use the hostility which he has transferred to the analyst as a means of keeping positive transference feelings at bay. Here the patient employs his hostile transference feelings to protect himself against emerging and threatening positive (usually erotic) transferences. Moreover, that aspect of the positive transference which 'is present . . . from the beginning of treatment' is different in quality from the erotic transferences which arise during the course of treatment (1912a). The former can be regarded as a component of the treatment alliance, previously discussed in Chapter 3.

Freud suggested that the particular characteristics of a patient's transference stem from the specific features of that patient's neurosis, and are not simply an outcome of the analytic process and common to all patients (1912a). The specific qualities of a patient's transference were given a further meaning when the concept of 'transference neurosis' was introduced (Freud, 1914a). This emphasized the way in which the earlier relationships which

* The relation of transference to *resistance* is dealt with in Chap. 7. The 'transference-cure' can be distinguished from a 'flight into health' which can be regarded as a form of resistance.

were components of the neurosis itself also mould the dominating pattern of the patient's feelings towards the psychoanalyst. The 'transference neurosis' concept was amplified by Freud (1920) when he commented that the patient in analysis is

> 'obliged to *repeat* the repressed material as a contemporary experience instead of, as the physician would prefer to see, *remembering* it as something belonging to the past. These reproductions which emerge with such unwished-for exactitude, always have as their subject some portion of infantile sexual life . . . and they are invariably acted out in the sphere of the transference, of the patient's relation to the physician. When things have reached this stage, it may be said that the earlier neurosis has now been replaced by a fresh, "transference neurosis".'*

The repetition of the past in the form of contemporary transferences was seen by Freud as a consequence of the (inappropriately named) 'compulsion to repeat' (1920).†

In order to put later developments into perspective, it is necessary to point out that the concept of transference was elaborated by Freud during the years in which mental functioning was largely thought of by Freud and his colleagues in terms of the

---

* It is unfortunate that the term 'transference neurosis' as used by Freud is so close to the label which he applied to a whole class of psychiatric *disorders* – the so-called 'transference neuroses', i.e. those disorders in which transference phenomena could be observed. In his earlier writings he showed his belief that these could be distinguished from other types of disorder, the 'narcissistic neuroses', in which transference phenomena were not thought to develop readily. The latter group corresponds to what we would now refer to as the functional psychoses. Most psychoanalysts now believe that transference phenomena occur in patients belonging to both groups. However, it should be said that Freud thought that the transference neurosis could occur characteristically in the psychoanalytic treatment of patients suffering from the 'transference neuroses', i.e. conversion hysteria, anxiety hysteria and obsessional neurosis (1916–17). A great deal of confusion attaches to the term transference neurosis (Kepecs, 1966).

† The 'repetition-compulsion' is inappropriately named in that it implies an explanation for the observation that people tend to repeat earlier (usually childhood) patterns over and over again. Psychoanalysts have often tended to elevate descriptive concepts to the status of explanatory principles. Moreover, the tendency to repeat is not a 'compulsion' in the psychiatric sense of the term.

vicissitudes of the instinctual drives and of the energies which were thought to propel them. Freud conceived of sexual wishes towards an important figure of the past as an investment ('cathexis') of sexual drive energy ('libido') in the image of the person (the 'libidinal object') concerned. Transference was thought of as the displacement of libido from the memory of the original object to the person of the analyst, who became the new object of the patient's sexual wishes, the patient being unaware of this process of displacement from the past.

The increasing emphasis on the analysis of transference, together with developments in ego psychology (see Chap. 1), have led other psychoanalytic writers to attempt to refine and expand the concept in order to achieve a clearer understanding of clinical phenomena and to integrate the concept of transference with developments in theoretical formulations in regard to the functioning of the ego. The history of the development of the concept of transference is a prime example of the problems which are engendered when a concept which developed during an early phase of psychoanalysis is maintained, in its original form, when newer theoretical developments have taken place. Anna Freud, in her book *The Ego and the Mechanisms of Defence* (1936) proposed a differentiation of transference phenomena in which transference, as described by Freud, represented one main category.

A second type of transference was described as 'transference of defence'. She included in the latter group of transferences the repetition of the measures which the patient had taken, early in his life, to protect himself against the painful consequences of childhood sexual and aggressive wishes. An example of this would be the patient who develops, during the course of his analysis, an attitude of belligerent rejection of the analyst, transferring here an attitude which he had taken up in childhood in order to protect himself against feelings of love and affection, because he feared that these would lead him into danger. Such a formulation extends the earlier and simpler view of Freud in which the 'defensive' hostility would be seen, not as a repetition of a defensive measure of childhood, a repetition of a mode of ego functioning, but rather as the employment of existing hostile feelings to protect the individual against the consequences of his emerging positive transference.

Anna Freud further differentiated 'acting in the transference', in which the transference intensified and spilled over into the

41

patient's daily life. Thus feelings and wishes towards the analyst, aroused during the course of treatment, might be enacted towards other people in the patient's current environment. 'Acting in the transference' is close to the concept of *acting out* to be discussed in Chapter 9.

At the same time, Anna Freud added a further category which she regarded as a sub-species of transference, and which she believed should be kept separate from transference proper. She referred here to *externalizations*, exemplified by the patient who feels guilty and, instead of experiencing the pangs of conscience, expects the analyst's reproaches. This externalization of a formed part of the personality was thought to be different from the repetition, in the transference, of the patient's childhood relationships towards, for example, a punitive father. A further example of externalization would be that of the patient who develops the belief (or fear) that the analyst wishes to seduce him, such a belief being based upon the externalization or, in this case, the particular form of externalization usually known as 'projection', on to the analyst of the patient's own sexual feelings towards him. What is 'externalized' is the patient's unconscious sexual desires, and this need not necessarily be regarded as the repetition of an infantile defensive manoeuvre. The distinction between externalization and transference 'proper' has not been systematically pursued by later writers, although it is of interest that both Alexander (1925) and Freud (1940) referred to the psychoanalyst 'taking over' the role of the patient's conscience (or 'superego'), and saw this as being an important part of the therapeutic process.*

* It should be understood that at this time neither Alexander nor Freud implied that the analyst actively strove to take over this role – rather, he found it thrust upon him by the patient's externalization. In such instances (and this is true for all other forms of transference as well) it is precisely the analyst's refusal to act in the role in which he is cast which can be regarded as the basis for interpretation aimed at changing the patient's patterns of functioning. However, Alexander later, in the developments of psychoanalysis attempted by the Chicago school, suggested that the analyst could actively modify the expression of his own behaviour and attitudes in order not to fit in with the externalizations and transferences of the patient. This was one of the innovations suggested by Alexander in pursuit of the 'corrective emotional experience'. As Alexander put it (1948) '. . . the principle of corrective emotional

There has been a strong tendency, within psychoanalysis, towards a widening of the transference concept. This can be traced in part to two trends in psychoanalysis which found their expression in the so-called 'English school' of psychoanalysis. James Strachey (1934) had suggested that the only effective interpretations in psychoanalytic treatment were transference interpretations and, as a consequence, analysts who were influenced by his views chose to formulate as many of their interpretations as possible in transference terms, in order to increase the effectiveness of their interventions. The second trend was represented by the theoretical formulations of Melanie Klein who, as a consequence of her analytic work with children, came to view all later behaviour as being very largely a repetition of relationships which she considered to obtain in the first year of life (1932). The combination of these trends resulted in a tendency for some analysts to regard all communications brought by the patient as indicating the transference of early infantile relationships, and to refrain from comments which did not refer to the transference features of the relationship between the patient and the analyst. This tendency has been fully discussed by Zetzel (1956). Many analysts have contributed to the extension of the transference concept. For example, Edward Glover (1937) emphasized that 'an adequate conception of transference must reflect the *totality* of the individual's development . . . he displaces on to the analyst not merely affects and ideas but *all* he has ever learnt or forgotten throughout his mental development'.

While some authorities have extended the concept within the psychoanalytic situation, others (while not accepting that all aspects of the patient's relationship to his analyst should be regarded as transference) have taken the view, in line with a comment of Freud's on the ubiquity of transference (1909a), that transference should be regarded as a general psychological phenomenon. Thus Greenson (1965a) writes:

'Transference is the experiencing of feelings, drives, attitudes, fantasies and defences towards a person in the present which are inappropriate to that person and are a repetition, a displacement

experience is a consciously planned regulation of the therapist's own emotional responses to the patient's material (counter-transference) in such a way as to counteract the harmful effects of the parental attitudes'.

43

of reactions originating in regard to significant persons of early childhood. I emphasize [says Greenson] that for a reaction to be considered transference it must have two characteristics: it must be a repetition of the past and it must be inappropriate to the present.'

Such a definition appears to include more than Freud had originally intended. For example, it would include habitual types of reacting to other persons which have become part of the patient's character (e.g. a tendency to be afraid of authority), and which might be regarded as inappropriate to the present. This is quite different from the conception of transference as the development, during the process of the psychoanalytic work, of feelings which were not apparent at the beginning of treatment, but which emerged as a consequence of the conditions of treatment.

Because of the belief that the extensions of the concept made by many psychoanalytic writers must lead to lesser rather than greater clarity, a return to a more limited view of transference has been advocated by a number of authors. Waelder (1956) has suggested that the concept of transference should be restricted to occurrences within the classical psychoanalytic situation. He says:

'Transference may be said to be an attempt of the patient to revive and re-enact, in the analytic situation and in relation to the analyst, situations and fantasies of his childhood. Hence transference is a regressive process. . . . Transference develops in consequence of the conditions of the analytic experiment, viz., of the analytic situation and the analytic technique.'

More recently, in a very full discussion of the divergent trends in regard to the transference concept, Loewenstein (1969) concludes that 'transference outside of analysis obviously cannot be described in identical terms with the transferences which appear during and due to the analytic process.' Loewenstein arrived at this view because of his conviction that the two aspects of transference seen in analysis, i.e. resistance and the vehicle for discovery and cure, exist exclusively in the analytic situation and can never be observed outside it.

It seems clear that different psychoanalytic authors have advocated rather different definitions of transference. The meaning of the term varies according to the context in which it is used, and it is apparent that if the term is to be used in a broad sense, sub-categories need to be distinguished. At present the term 'transference' is used by different psychoanalysts in some or all of the following senses:

(1) To include what we have discussed as the treatment alliance (Chap. 3).
(2) To denote the emergence of infantile feelings and attitudes in a new form, directed towards the person of the analyst, essentially as described by Freud (1895, 1905b, 1909a, 1912a, 1914a, 1916–17, 1920).
(3) To include 'transference of defence' and 'externalizations' (A. Freud, 1936).
(4) To encompass all 'inappropriate' thoughts, attitudes, fantasies and emotions which are revivals of the past and which the patient may display (whether he is conscious of them or not) in relation to the analyst. This would include such things as the patient's initial 'irrational' anxieties about coming to treatment and particular attitudes towards people which form part of his personality structure, and which also show themselves towards the analyst (Greenson, 1965a).*
(5) To include *all* aspects of the patient's relationship to his analyst. This view of transference sees every aspect of the patient's involvement with the analyst as being a repetition of past (usually very early) relationships. Indeed, *every* verbal and non-verbal communication or expression by the patient during the course of his analysis is regarded as transference. Analysts who take this view of transference regard all the patient's associations as essentially referring to some thought or feeling about the analyst (e.g. Rosenfeld, 1965a).

It would seem that the argument (Waelder, 1956; Loewenstein, 1969) that the concept of transference should be limited to the psychoanalytic situation alone is unnecessary, although it is possible to understand the motive which prompts such a limitation,

* Greenson nevertheless distinguishes transference from the 'working alliance' (1965a) and from the 'real' relationship of the patient to his analyst (Greenson and Wexler, 1969). Szasz has attempted to discuss the logical difficulties which arise in the distinction between transference and 'reality' (1963).

i.e. the increasing tendency to the wide and indiscriminate application of the term 'transference'. However, it is clear that the same
phenomena which occur in psychoanalytic treatment can occur
outside it. Freud put it thus: 'It is not a fact that transference
emerges with greater intensity during psychoanalysis than outside
it. In institutions in which nerve patients are treated non-
analytically, we can observe transference occurring with the
greatest intensity' (1912a). It has been emphasized, however, that
the classical analytical situation does appear to provide conditions
which foster the development of transferences, and which enable
the phenomena to be examined in relatively uncontaminated forms
(Stone, 1961).

At the other extreme, the widest use of the concept, in which
all communications and behaviour within the psychoanalytic
setting are regarded as transference, seems to remove all value
from the concept if it is to be extended outside psychoanalytic
treatment, for it would then follow that all behaviour could be
described as transference, i.e. determined by the tendency to
repeat past patterns of behaviour and experience. While it is true
that aspects of past reactions and even infantile experiences will
tend to be repeated in the present, and that present reality will
tend to be perceived in terms of the past, there are also factors which
oppose this distortion (so-called 'reality-testing'). It seems likely
that the relative lack of opportunity to 'test' reality in the psychoanalytic treatment situation allows transference distortions to
develop readily and to be seen most clearly. In ordinary human
relationships, the person towards whom a transference is made
often acts in such a way as to correct the distorted transference
perception which has arisen. However, he may also allow himself
to accept the transference role which may have been thrust upon
him, and to act in accordance with it (see Chap. 6). The analyst
thus both provides an opportunity for transference distortions by
not 'feeding back' reality in order to correct the patient's mis-
perception, and does not accept the role enjoined upon him by the
patient's transference, thus enabling the irrational determinants
of the transference to be explored.

An intermediate view between these two extremes is taken by
Sandler *et al* (1969). On the basis of an examination of child
psychoanalytic material, these authors reject the notion that all the
material of the analytic patient can be regarded as transference,

46

but stress instead that the very concept of transference as a unitary or 'unidimensional' phenomenon may impede the understanding of what is happening in the relationship between the patient and his analyst. They suggest that the analyst should not think solely in terms of what is transference and what is not, but should rather examine the many different aspects of relationships as they arise within the analysis, and towards the person of the analyst. The point is made that if the clinical concept of transference is to be understood from the point of view of general psychology, relationships in general have to be studied. Transference is a special clinical manifestation of the many different components of normal relationships. The authors stress that the special psychoanalytic situation may facilitate the emergence of particular aspects of relationships, especially aspects of past relationships, but emphasize that it is technically of the greatest importance to distinguish between these various elements rather than to regard *all* aspects of the patient's relationship to the analyst as being a repetition of past relationships to important figures.

It seems important to distinguish between the general tendency to repeat past relationships in the present (e.g. as can be observed in persisting character traits such as 'demandingness', 'provocativeness', 'intolerance of authority', and the like) and a *process* characterized by the development of feelings and attitudes towards another person (or an institution) which represent a concentration of a past attitude or feeling, inappropriate to the present, and directed *quite specifically* towards the other person or institution. From this point of view, the anxieties which a patient might have on entering treatment need not be regarded as transference, even though they may be a repetition of some earlier and important experience. On the other hand, a patient who has been in treatment for some time may develop fears about coming to treatment, fears which are now believed and felt by the patient to be a function of the specific qualities of the therapist, even though there may be little foundation in reality for such transference beliefs and feelings. In this sense, transference can be regarded as *a specific illusion* which develops in regard to the other person, one which, unbeknown to the subject, represents, in some of its features, a repetition of a relationship towards an important figure in the person's past. It should be emphasized that this is

47

felt by the subject, not as a repetition of the past, but as strictly appropriate to the present and to the particular person involved.

It should be added that transference need not be restricted to the illusory apperception of another person in the sense in which it is described here, but can be taken to include the unconscious (and often subtle) attempts to manipulate or to provoke situations with others which are a concealed repetition of earlier experiences and relationships. It has been pointed out previously that when such transference manipulations or provocations occur in ordinary life, the person towards whom they are directed may either show that he does not accept the role, or may, if he is unconsciously disposed in that direction, in fact accept it, and act accordingly. It is likely that such acceptance or rejection of a transference role is not based on a conscious awareness of what is happening, but rather on unconscious cues. Transference elements enter to a varying degree into all relationships, and these (e.g. choice of spouse or employer) are often determined by some characteristic of the other person who (consciously or unconsciously) represents some attribute of an important figure of the past.

It would seem to be useful to differentiate transference from non-transference elements, rather than to label all elements in the relationship (arising from the side of the patient) as transference. This may lead to greater precision in defining the clinically important elements in a whole variety of situations and elucidating the relative roles of the many factors which enter into the interaction between patient and therapist in any form of treatment.

Chapter 5

Special Forms of Transference

The concept of transference, as developed by Freud, arose within the context of the psychoanalytic treatment of neurotic patients. The extension of the techniques of psychoanalysis to a wider range of patients, including psychotics, has led to the introduction of a number of terms to describe special and additional forms of transference. This chapter is concerned with aspects of the relationship between patient and doctor which are discussed in the literature under such headings as 'Erotic Transference' (Saul, 1962), 'Erotized Transference' (E. Rappaport, 1956; Greenson, 1967), 'Transference Psychosis' (Rosenfeld, 1952, 1954, 1969; Searles, 1961, 1963; Wallerstein, 1967) and 'Delusional Transference' (Little, 1958, 1960a, 1966; Hammett, 1961).

In the previous chapter, we were concerned with transference in the forms in which it normally develops. Following a review of the main trends in the literature it was seen that the concept was understood and applied in a number of different ways. We concluded that a useful statement of the transference concept would be to regard it as:

'a specific illusion which develops in regard to the other person, one which, unbeknown to the subject, represents, in some of its features, a repetition of a relationship towards an important figure in the person's past. It should be emphasized that this is felt by the subject, not as a repetition of the past, but as strictly appropriate to the present and to the particular person involved.'

We added that 'transference need not be restricted to the illusory apperception of another person . . . but can be taken to include the unconscious (and often subtle) attempts to manipulate or to provoke situations with others which are a concealed repetition of earlier experiences and relationships'.

The literature which has grown around the special forms of transference discussed in this chapter implies, fairly consistently, that the phenomena described are some form of repetition of past psychological situations or relationships, occurring in the course of psychoanalysis or psychoanalytically orientated psychotherapy, and can consequently be regarded as transference. However, these transferences have the quality of appearing so grossly unrealistic and inappropriate in comparison with 'ordinary' transferences as to warrant special designation. Authors writing on these topics usually regard these 'special' transference phenomena as consequences of a regressive revival of primitive relationships, thought to occur either as a consequence of the patient's psychopathology or because the regression is fostered by the particular characteristics of the psychoanalytic treatment situation (or as a consequence of both). Whereas it is generally accepted by psychoanalysts that psychoanalytic treatment normally creates suitable conditions for regression – and some analysts (e.g. Waelder, 1956) link the normal development of transference with regression in the analytic situation – the extent of the regression, and its particular form in certain types of patient, is regarded as leading to special forms of transference. Many psychoanalysts subscribe to the view that severe psychiatric disturbances, in particular the psychoses, can be seen as regressively-revived repetitions of earlier, infantile states. By some (e.g. Klein, 1948), these early states are regarded as being 'psychotic'. Other psychoanalysts (e.g. Arlow and Brenner, 1964, 1969) consider that the major effect of regressive processes in producing psychotic states is on the more organized parts of the personality, i.e. on the ego and superego. Arlow and Brenner put it thus (1964):

' . . . the great majority of the alterations in the ego and superego functions which characterize the psychoses are part of the individual's defensive efforts in situations of inner conflict and are motivated by a need to avoid the emergence of anxiety, just as is the case in normal and in neurotic conflicts. In the psychoses the defensive alterations in ego functions are often so extensive as to disrupt the patient's relationship with the world about him to a serious degree.'

Erotic Transference and Eroticized (or Erotized) Transference

In 1915 Freud described certain cases of 'transference love' in which the patient undergoing psychoanalytic treatment declared herself to be 'in love' with the analyst (1915a). Such patients may refuse to carry on the usual work of treatment, may reject interpretations relating the present feelings to the past, and seek no further enlightenment as to the meaning and cause of the symptoms of which they had previously complained. The analytic sessions are used for the expression of love, for gratification through the presence of the beloved, and these patients beseech the analyst for a return of their love. Although Freud did not necessarily regard such patients as suffering from unusually severe neurotic disturbances, and did not see the emergence of this form of transference as an inevitable contra-indication to psychoanalytic therapy, he suggested that sometimes a transfer to another analyst might be necessary. He spoke of such patients as possessing 'an elemental passionateness', as being 'children of nature'.

It seems that in the course of time psychoanalysts have not come to expect their patients to fall in love with them so frequently and to such a degree, or are perhaps more skilled in seeing and interpreting the occurrence of such feelings as a form of resistance (see Chap. 7) against other, less acceptable feelings and impulses.* However, when it does occur to the extent that there is an intense demand for gratification, and productive analytic work ceases, then serious psychopathology is thought to be present. Alexander (1950) has drawn attention to the problem of the dependent patient, both demanding love and wishing to give it. Blitzsten (whose unpublished remarks are quoted by Rappaport, 1956, and Greenson, 1967) is regarded as the first to have linked a highly sexualized attitude to the doctor with serious pathology. Rappaport (1956), in an extensive discussion of the subject, comments that 'Blitzsten noted that in a transference situation the analyst is seen "as if" he were the parent, while in erotization of the transference "he is"† the parent. The patient does not even

---

* In our own experience, patients who habitually 'sexualize' (through flirtation and subtle sexual provocation), particularly those with a so-called 'hysterical character', are often found to be defending against the possibility of becoming depressed.

† A form of over-statement not uncommon in psychoanalytic writings. This statement probably reflects the analyst's feeling that he is treated

51

acknowledge the "as if".' The difficulties inherent in such a formulation are obvious, and we shall return to this point later.

Rappaport suggests that such patients, who overplay the erotic
component in the transference 'insist unequivocally, from the
very beginning, that they want the analyst to behave toward them
as the parent'. The patients are not embarrassed or ashamed by
such wishes. They express their anger openly when the analyst
does not comply with their demands. Rappaport correlates such
intensely sexual demanding reactions in analysis with the severity
of the patient's pathology. 'Such an erotization of transference
corresponding to a severe disturbance of the sense of reality is
indicative of the severity of the illness. These patients are not
neurotics, they are "borderline" cases or ambulatory schizophrenics.' He comments that 'though the analytic situation is
especially liable to such distortion, these patients try to convert
every significant person into a parent'.

Rappaport, in expressing his agreement with Blitzsten that for
such patients the analyst *is* the parent, nevertheless does not
maintain that these patients are deluded or hallucinated to the
degree that the analyst is *believed to be* the actual parent. However,
it seems clear that there is a special quality to their transferences.
Here the transference is not hidden, 'the patient screams out that
he wants his fantasy to be reality'. The patient believes that in his
analyst he can get a parent (presumably someone who will *act
and be like* a real or wished-for parent in the patient's life). The
view of the analyst *qua* analyst is completely lost.

It could be argued that this does not reflect transference at all.
In 1951 Nunberg put forward the view that the patient's attempts
to transform the analyst into the parent do not constitute transference. He spoke of a patient whose 'particular fixation to her
father created the wish to find his reincarnation in the person of
the analyst, and, since her desire to transform the latter into a
person *identical* with her father could not be fulfilled, the attempts
to establish a working transference were futile'. If this patient had
projected unconscious images of her past objects onto the person
of the analyst, then, in Nunberg's view, we would be dealing with
transference. However, 'She did not project the image of her

very much like a parent might be, without the quality of 'as if' existing
to the same degree as with his other patients.

father on to the analyst; she tried to change her analyst according to the image of her father.' Clearly Nunberg is referring to phenomena similar to those described by Rappaport. Moreover, in the previous chapter on transference (Chap. 4) we spoke of the 'concealed' repetition of earlier experiences and relationships in the transference, implying that the patient is not aware of the repetition of the past in the present. While this would argue against the use of the term 'transference' in regard to the phenomena described by Rappaport, it is equally possible for a patient to have an erotized transference of this sort without being aware that a repetition of the past is involved.

Rappaport's main theme relates to the management of the patient who wishes to give sexual love to, and to receive it from, a therapist. Such technical considerations are the central concern of a paper by Saul (1962). He connects this type of transference, more specifically than Rappaport, with real frustration in relationships in early life, suggesting that the hostility and anger engendered by such frustration may also be repeated in relation to the person of the therapist. In addition, the extreme love is postulated to be, in part, a means of protecting the doctor from hostile feelings. The hostility and destructiveness in such patients has been noted by others (e.g. Nunberg, 1951; Greenson, 1967). Greenson relates the erotic transference to other areas of disturbance, and comments: 'Patients who suffer from what is called an "eroticized" transference are prone to very destructive acting out. . . . All these patients have transference resistances that stem from underlying impulses of hatred. They seek only to discharge these feelings and oppose the analytic work.' In speaking of his own experience of such cases he comments that 'they came to the hours eagerly, but not for insight, only to enjoy the physical proximity. My interventions seemed irrelevant to them.' Greenson considers such patients to be unsuitable for classical psychoanalytic treatment. In his view they cannot tolerate the demands of classical psychoanalysis (cf. also Wexler, 1960), and cannot maintain an adequate treatment alliance.

Transference in Psychotics, Transference Psychosis and Delusional Transference
The work of Rappaport (1956), Wallerstein (1967) and Greenson (1967) appears to refer to forms of transference intermediate

53

between the cases discussed by Freud and the cases of psychotic transference or transference psychosis described by such authors as Rosenfeld (1952, 1954, 1969) and Searles (1961, 19ս3), in which frankly psychotic features appear in the patient's relationship to his therapist.

We have pointed out in Chapter 4 that Freud (1911a, 1914b) took the view that transference did not occur in what he called the 'narcissistic neuroses' (functional psychoses). He believed that psychotic psychopathology represented a return, in part, to a very early level of psychological functioning, a level at which the capacity to relate to and to love others as distinct from oneself had not developed. The withdrawal of interest in the outside world in psychotics was thought of as an outcome of a return (regression) to the early 'narcissistic' level. Abraham (1908) also believed that transference phenomena were absent in schizophrenia.

As Rosenfeld (1952, 1969) has shown, beginning with Nunberg's observations (1920) of transference phenomena in a patient with catatonic schizophrenia, an increasing number of psychoanalysts have disputed Freud's original contention and have made the point that transference does occur in psychotics. Notable among these have been Harry Stack Sullivan (1931), Federn (1943) and Rosen (1946). More recently, Searles (1961, 1963), Rosenfeld (1952, 1965a, 1969) and Balint (1968) have, from their different theoretical viewpoints, denied that the earliest stages of psychological development (which they believe to be recapitulated in aspects of the symptoms of schizophrenic patients) are free from the investment of emotional interest in others. Thus Rosenfeld comments (1952) 'we are dealing here not with an absence of transference, but with the difficult problem of recognizing and intepreting schizophrenic transference-phenomena'. He ascribes this difficulty to the fact that 'as soon as the schizophrenic approaches *any* object in love or hate he seems to become confused with this object . . . [which] throws some light on the infant's difficulty in distinguishing between the "me" and the "not me".' The view that misidentifications and delusional ideas develop within the psychotic's relation to his doctor is extended and elaborated by Searles (1963), Little (1960a) and Balint (1968). Balint appears to be the only one of these authors who is alert to the dangers of reconstructing early psychological functioning on

54

the basis of it being exactly like the behaviour of disturbed adults in psychoanalytic therapy.

It seems very likely that the transference concept can legitimately be applied to aspects of the psychotic patient's interaction with his therapist. Even the most withdrawn catatonic schizophrenic may, after recovery of rationality, show evidence of considerable perceptiveness of events involving others at the time of his illness. Moreover, there is little doubt that some disturbed behaviour arises in response to perceptions of others. (In this context, the social psychiatric surveys of Brown *et al* (1966), which show that the symptomatology of schizophrenia has cultural determinants, are relevant.) Doctors and ward personnel alike are taken into the content of disordered thought processes. What Searles, Rosenfeld and others (e.g. Fromm-Reichmann, 1950) seek to show by their detailed case presentations is that such thought processes represent repetitions of earlier interpersonal relationships. Searles writes of the chronic schizophrenic patient (1963) 'He is so incompletely differentiated in his ego-functioning that he tends to feel not that the therapist reminds him of, or is like, his mother or father (or whomever, from his early life) but rather his functioning towards the therapist is couched in the unscrutinized assumption that the therapist *is* the mother or father.' But he adds, in line with Rosenfeld, that 'one of the great reasons for our underestimating the role of transference is that it may require a very long time for the transference to become not only sufficiently differentiated but also sufficiently integrated, sufficiently coherent, to be identifiable'.

Just as Freud thought that in the treatment of neurotic patients the internal problems which give rise to the neurosis become concentrated within the analytic treatment situation as a 'transference neurosis' (1914b, 1920), so Rosenfeld and Searles believe that a parallel 'transference psychosis' can be discerned. Searles (1963) designates four varieties of transference psychosis:

1. Transference situations in which the therapist feels unrelated to the patient.
2. Situations in which a clear-cut relatedness has been established between patient and therapist, and the therapist no longer feels unrelated to the patient; but the relatedness is a deeply ambivalent one.

55

3. Instances in which the patient's psychosis represents, in the transference, an effort to complement the therapist's personality, or to help the 'therapist-parent' to become established as a separate and whole person.

4. Situations where a chronically and deeply disturbed patient tries to get the therapist to do his thinking for him, but at the same time tries to get away from such a close relationship.

Searles is here emphasizing counter-transference perceptions by the doctor as a basis for assessing the type of psychotic disturbance (see Chap. 6). He relates each of the types of 'transference psychosis' to actually damaging (although perhaps misperceived and misinterpreted) family patterns. Here he allies himself with the 'family theorists' of schizophrenia (Wynne and Singer, 1963; Bateson *et al*, 1956; Lidz *et al*, 1965; Mishler and Waxler, 1966). Rosenfeld suggests that what is reproduced in the treatment situation is not an actual parent-child situation but a version of that situation which had been distorted by the infant's fantasy.

There does not, in our view, appear to be sufficient evidence that the *content* of the psychotic's transference is characteristic or specific. The evidence that the psychotic can relate to people (albeit in a psychotic way) is strong, as is the evidence that aspects of childhood relationships, whether these be real or fantasied, enter into the content of the transference. Nor is there reason to doubt the observation that the psychotic's relationship to his therapist may become extremely intense, and the concept of 'transference psychosis' may in this context be a useful one.* What seems to be the distinguishing feature in the transference of psychotic patients is the *form* which it takes, a form which is closely related to the psychotic mental state of the patient. A transference wish which might be resisted in the neurotic, or produced in a disguised form, might find expression as a delusional conviction in the psychotic. From a psychoanalytic point

---

* The fact that transferences occur in psychotic patients, that these transferences can be interpreted, and that the patient may react to transference interpretations, has led certain analysts (e.g. Rosenfeld and Searles) to conclude that psychotic patients can be more effectively treated by psychoanalytic methods than by other techniques. In our view, the evidence for this is unconvincing, although it appears to be true that close daily contact with a therapist can bring about an improvement in the chronic psychotic's condition.

56

of view the differences could be attributed to defective functioning of the controlling and organizing part of the personality (the ego), in particular those functions connected with distinguishing 'real' from 'imaginary'. To put it very simply, everything which has been described in regard to the form of the transference in psychotics can be attributed to the general features of the psychosis. If parts of the schizophrenic patient's personality are relatively intact, then we can expect that aspects of his behaviour and attitudes based on those parts may remain intact. This would appear to be the basis for the capacity for certain psychotic patients to establish a treatment alliance of some sort. This capacity to form a treatment alliance may only exist in regard to particular forms of treatment, and its assessment must inevitably determine the choice of therapeutic method.

Thus far we have been concerned, in this section of the chapter, with the concepts of psychotic transference and transference psychosis as forms found in psychotic patients. There is a completely different usage of the term 'transference psychosis' in the literature. In 1912 Ferenczi described transitory psychotic or near-psychotic symptoms occurring during the analytic session in patients who were not otherwise psychotic. These included, in rare cases, true hallucinations evoked in the analytic hour. In 1957 Reider published a paper on 'Transference Psychosis' in which he described the appearance of psychotic and delusional features in the transference of a non-psychotic patient. The literature on this topic has been ably summarized by Wallerstein (1967) who, like Reider, confined the usage of the term to 'patients deemed wholly within the neurotic range in terms of character structure and adjudged appropriate for classical analysis, in whom nevertheless a disorganizing reaction of psychotic intensity occurred within the transference'. Such symptoms as delusional hypochondriasis (Atkins, 1967), 'delusional' fantasies (Wallerstein, 1967) and paranoid delusional states (Romm, 1957) are most commonly described. While it may be possible to attribute the appearance of these psychotic features to the regression-inducing qualities of the analytic situation, they nevertheless only appear in certain patients. The concept of a transitory psychotic mental 'posture' might be useful here (Hill, 1968; Sandler and Joffe, 1970). By 'posture' in this connection is meant the particular organization or constellation of ego functions and defence mechanisms which the

57

patient might adopt in order to deal with a situation which is extremely dangerous or painful. Usually this will be regressive, i.e. will be a return to an earlier mode of functioning. With the disappearance of the painful state, or the threat to the patient, he may be able to resume a more adult mental 'posture'.

Little (1958) and Hammett (1961) make use of the term 'delusional transference' to describe a situation in which gross anomalies of the patient-therapist relationship develop; they consider that what is observed is a distorted but nonetheless discernible recapitulation of aspects of very early mother-child relationships. The problems posed by the assumption (made by a number of authors) of phases of 'childhood psychosis' as explanations of psychotic-like beliefs arising during analysis have been mentioned earlier and have been discussed by Frosch (1967).

A number of analysts, including Winnicott (1954, 1955), Khan (1960) and Little (1960a, 1966) have advised that the analyst should, with some patients, permit the development of disturbed (and disturbing) infantile dependent behaviour and of associated intense and primitive feelings. They have suggested (with Balint, 1968) that only in such states is it possible to relieve and hence undo earlier failures of maternal care. This latter-day version of the so-called 'corrective emotional experience' (Alexander and French, 1946) is not accepted as a valid technical approach by many analysts.

The Distinguishing Features of the 'Special' Forms of Transference
The notion of repetition of the past appears to be common to all concepts of transference, but it is clear that the form in which the past is reproduced may show substantial variation. In the 'ordinary' transferences of neurotic and 'normal' patients, the capacity to test the transference illusion against reality exists, and the patient is able to view himself to some extent as if he were another person. Interpretations which take the form of 'you are reacting to me *as if* I were your father' are normally understood by the patient who can bring his reasonable and self-observing capacities to bear on what is happening. In such cases the patient possesses and employs the elements which make for a successful treatment alliance (Chap. 3).

In the special forms of transference described in this chapter, the patient either does not possess or does not use these self-critical and self-scrutinizing elements, and it is of interest that writers on both the erotic and psychotic forms of transference refer to the disappearance of the 'as if' quality of the transference. In our view what distinguishes such types of transference from the more usual forms is *the patient's attitude towards his own behaviour*. The same transference content may emerge in the analysis of a neurotic, who may bring it in a roundabout way (e.g. via a dream), while patients who are psychotic (even if only appearing temporarily so during the analytic hour) bring it more directly, perhaps in the form of a delusional belief. The difference would appear to reside in the formal aspects of the current mental state of the patient.

Statements to the effect that the patient with one or other form of erotic or psychotic transference sees and treats the analyst like the real parent could only be strictly correct if the patient held the delusional conviction that the analyst *was in fact* his parent. Cases of this sort must be extremely rare, but it would appear that what is meant by such statements is that the patient loses sight of the professional role and function of the therapist, and is unable to maintain a normal 'distance' from, and the capacity for insight into, what has been going on. Further, it should be noted that the content of the transference, whatever its form, should not be regarded as a simple repetition of the past. Thus a patient who develops a homosexual transference towards his analyst may react, if he is a neurotic, with anxiety and resistance. If he is psychotic, he might react with delusions of persecution. In both cases he would be defending against the same unacceptable impulses and wishes in himself.

It is impressive that the varieties of transference content described by certain psychoanalytic authors (e.g. Rosenfeld, 1965a) in regard to schizophrenia are extremely similar to those that may be found in psychoses which are undoubtedly of organic origin. This lends support to the view that psychotic productions, including transference manifestations of the sort discussed in this chapter, are not a consequence of a need to repeat inadequately-resolved infantile psychotic states. It seems to us perfectly plausible to say that the distinguishing features in different types of transference relate to the way in which unconscious thoughts, impulses and wishes, which might partly originate in childhood, tend to come into consciousness, and the way in which they are accepted, rejected, acted upon or modified. It would seem likely, therefore, that the specific defects which lead to psychosis and to psychotic transferences lie in such areas as the controlling, organizing, synthesizing, analysing and perceptual functions of the personality. This view would allow us to understand why psychotic transferences can emerge in certain patients with organic brain disease.

There may well be particular family situations which predispose subjects at risk to schizophrenic breakdown. The 'double bind' phenomenon (Bateson *et al*, 1956) is certainly observable, and the patient may attempt to recreate it with the therapist in the transference relationship. However, similar modes of relating are seen in families which do not contain a schizophrenic member.

In the last chapter, we suggested that the concept of transference was capable of extension outside the classical psychoanalytic situation, and that the differentiation between transference and non-transference elements in any patient-doctor relationship would be useful clinically. Similarly, the various special forms of transference discussed in this chapter may be observed outside psychoanalysis, and can often be traced in a whole variety of relationships. There appears to be ample clinical evidence to conclude that erotization of transference elements can occur outside the psychoanalytic situation, that psychotic patients can show psychotic and delusional features in their relations with others, and that special situations may produce or release transient psychotic reactions in certain individuals.

Chapter 6

Counter-Transference

In the previous three chapters we have discussed the *treatment alliance* and *transference*, concepts which have been used in connection with aspects of the relationship between the patient and his therapist. These two clinical concepts originated within the psychoanalytic treatment situation, and we have indicated the possibilities of extension outside it. Both concepts relate to and emphasize processes occurring within the patient, and tend to stress one side of the relationship only. Even the concept of treatment alliance, although nominally appearing to include the roles of both patient and therapist, has tended to be regarded from the point of view of processes and attitudes within the patient; the aspect of the therapist's attitudes, feelings and professional stance have, to a large extent, been omitted. However, in recent years more attention has been paid in psychoanalytic and other writings to the relation of the psychoanalyst towards his patient. Just as the term 'transference' is often used loosely as a synonym for the totality of the patient's relation to his therapist, so is the term 'counter-transference' often used in a general sense (both within psychoanalysis and outside it) to describe the whole of the therapist's feelings and attitudes towards his patient, and even to describe facets of ordinary non-therapeutic relationships (Kemper, 1966). Such a usage is very different from what was originally intended, and as a consequence confusion has arisen about the precise meaning of the term. It is the purpose of this chapter to examine the concept in the light of its origins and development within psychoanalysis, and to comment briefly on some possibilities of its extension outside the psychoanalytic treatment setting.

The term was first used by Freud in discussing the future prospects of psychoanalysis (1910a). He said of the psychoanalyst:

> 'We have become aware of the "counter-transference", which arises in him as a result of the patient's influence on his unconscious feelings, and we are almost inclined to insist that he shall recognize this counter-transference in himself and overcome it . . . no psychoanalyst goes further than his own complexes and internal resistances permit. . . . '

In the same year, in a letter to his colleague Ferenczi, whom he had analysed, he apologized for his failure to overcome counter-transference feelings which had interfered with Ferenczi's analysis (1910b).

Freud later developed the theme that the analyst should aim to show the patient as little as possible of his own personal life, and he warned analysts against discussing their own experiences and shortcomings with their patients. 'The doctor should be opaque to his patients, and, like a mirror, should show them nothing but what is shown to him.' He also pointed to the danger of falling into 'the temptation of projecting outwards some of the peculiarities of his own personality' (1912b).

Just as transference was, early on, seen by Freud as an obstruction to the patient's flow of free associations, so counter-transference was consistently regarded as an obstruction to the freedom of the analyst's understanding of the patient. In this context, Freud regarded the analyst's mind as an 'instrument' (1913b), its effective functioning in the analytic situation being impeded by counter-transference. Freud did not take the step (which he took in regard to transference) of regarding counter-transference as a useful tool in psychoanalytic work.

It should be emphasized that, for Freud, the fact that the psychoanalyst has feelings towards his patients, or conflicts aroused by his patients, did not in itself constitute counter-transference. He did not advocate that the analyst should turn into a 'mirror', but rather that he should aim to *function* like a mirror in the analytic situation, reflecting (through his interpretations) the meaning of the material brought by the patient, including the patient's transference distortions. Counter-transference was seen as a sort of 'resistance' in the psychoanalyst towards his patient, a resistance due to the arousal of unconscious conflicts by what the patient says, does or represents to the analyst. The analyst may, through self-scrutiny, become aware of the existence of such conflicts in himself, and this is an indication for him to make every effort to recognize their nature and to eliminate their adverse consequences. In Freud's view, the conflicts were not in themselves counter-transference, but could give rise to it.

Freud repeatedly stressed the limitations imposed on the analytic work by the analyst's psychological blind spots (1912b, 1915a, 1931, 1937a). He advocated initially (1910a) a continuous self-analysis for the analyst, but soon took the view that this was difficult because of the analyst's own resistances to self-understanding and recommended that the analyst undergo an analysis himself ('training analysis') in order to gain insight and to overcome the psychological deficiencies created by unresolved unconscious conflicts (1912a). Later, believing even this to be inadequate, he suggested that analysts be re-analysed about every five years (1937a).*

It is clear that Freud included in counter-transference more than the analyst's transference (in the sense in which he used the term) to his patient. While it is true that a patient may come to represent a figure of the analyst's past, counter-transference might arise simply because of the analyst's inability to deal appropriately with those aspects of the patient's communications and behaviour which impinge on inner problems of his own. Thus if a psychoanalyst had not resolved problems connected with his own aggression, for example, he might need to placate his patient whenever he detected aggressive feelings or thoughts towards him in the patient. Similarly, if the analyst is threatened by his own unconscious homosexual feelings, he may be unable to detect any homosexual implications in the patient's material; or, indeed, he may react with undue irritation to homosexual thoughts or wishes in the patient, may sidetrack the patient on to another topic, etc. The 'counter' in counter-transference may thus

* A recommendation which has not been commonly implemented, probably due to the fact that training analyses have become much longer and consequently more thorough. However, second analyses are not uncommon among psychoanalysts, especially if they perceive difficulties of their own in their work or outside it.

indicate a reaction in the analyst which implies a parallel to the patient's transference (as in 'counterpart') as well as being a reaction to them (as in 'counteract'). The etymology of the term has been discussed by Greenson (1967).

There have been a number of different lines of development in the psychoanalytic literature on counter-transference after Freud. Several authors have maintained that the term should be employed in the exact sense in which it was first used, i.e. that it should be limited to those unresolved conflicts and problems aroused in the psychoanalyst during the course of his work with the patient and which consequently hinder the analyst's effectiveness (Stern, 1924; Fliess, 1953). Thus Fliess says: 'counter-transference, always resistance, must always be analyzed'. Winnicott (1960) describes the counter-transference as the analyst's 'neurotic features *which spoil the professional attitude* and disturb the course of the analytic process as determined by the patient'. Others, while adhering more or less to the original concept, have emphasized that the origin of counter-transference hindrances lies predominantly in the therapist's transference towards the patient (A. Reich, 1951; Gitelson, 1952; Hoffer, 1956; Tower, 1956). For example, A. Reich remarks that the analyst

'may like or dislike the patient. As far as these attitudes are conscious, they have not yet anything to do with counter-transference. If these feelings increase in intensity, we can be fairly certain that the unconscious feelings of the analyst, his own transferences on to the patient, i.e. counter-transferences, are mixed in. . . . Counter-transference thus comprises the effects of the analyst's own unconscious needs and conflicts on his understanding or technique. In such cases the patient represents for the analyst an object of the past on to whom past feelings and wishes are projected . . . this is counter-transference in the proper sense' (1951).

Unfortunately the views of those authors who regard counter-transference as being the outcome of the analyst's own transference to the patient are often rendered obscure by their failure to indicate the exact sense in which they make use of the concept of transference (Chap. 4). Some appear to relate counter-transference to Freud's original concept of transference, while others equate it with all aspects of relationships (e.g. English and

Pearson, 1937). In line with this latter usage, M. Balint, in one of the earliest papers on counter-transference (1933), equated it with the analyst's own transference to his patient, and later (M. Balint and A. Balint, 1939) broadened the use of the term to include anything (even the disposition of the cushions on the couch) which reveals the personality of the analyst. In a later paper (1949) M. Balint uses the term counter-transference unambiguously to describe the totality of the analyst's attitudes and behaviour towards his patient. For Balint, unlike Freud, counter-transference has come to include the professional attitude of the analyst towards his patient.

A major development in psychoanalytic writings on counter-transference occurred when it began to be seen as a phenomenon of importance in helping the analyst to understand the hidden meaning of material brought by the patient. The essential idea put forward is that the analyst has elements of understanding and appreciation of the processes occurring in his patient, that these elements are not immediately conscious and that they can be discovered by the analyst if he monitors his own mental associations while listening to his patient. This is an idea which is implicit in descriptions by Freud of the value of the analyst's neutral or 'free-floating' attention (1909b, 1912b), but the first explicit statement of the positive value of counter-transference was made by Heimann (1950, 1960), and has been extended by others (e.g. Little, 1951, 1960b). Heimann began by regarding counter-transference as covering all the feelings which the analyst experiences towards his patient. The analyst has to be able to '*sustain* the feelings which are stirred up in him, as opposed to discharging them (as does the patient), in order to *subordinate* them to the analytic task in which he functions as the patient's mirror reflection'. Her basic assumption is 'that the analyst's unconscious understands that of his patient. This rapport on the deep level comes to the surface in the form of feelings which the analyst notices in response to his patient, in his "counter-transference" ' (1950). She maintains that the analyst must use his emotional response to the patient – his counter-transference – as a key to the understanding of the patient. In other words, an analyst may become aware of rising emotionally tinged reactions to a patient which cannot immediately be linked with the surface content of the patient's associations, but which nevertheless

65

indicate the existence of a role which is being unconsciously forced on to the analyst by the patient. The analyst's awareness of his own responses can thus provide an additional avenue of insight into the patient's unconscious mental processes. It is of some interest that this extension of the concept of counter-transference is similar to Freud's change in his view of the function of transference, first regarded only as a hindrance but later seen as an asset to therapy.

As with other psychoanalytic concepts, the attribution of additional meaning to the term 'counter-transference' has led to a loss of precision in its use. While there can be little doubt that the whole of the therapist's feelings towards his patient must be a subject of interest to those investigating the doctor-patient relationship in a variety of situations, it can be questioned whether the extension of the counter-transference concept to cover *all* the feelings experienced towards a patient is useful.

Most of the psychoanalytic literature on counter-transference appears to reflect adherence to one or other or both of the two main views described above, i.e. that counter-transference is either an obstacle to the analytic work or that it is a valuable tool. The problems arising from this have been recognized in the psychoanalytic literature (e.g. Orr, 1954). Kernberg, in a review of the writings on counter-transference (1965), has pointed out that the broadening of the term to include all emotional responses in the analyst is confusing and causes the term to lose all specific meaning. However, he also cites criticisms of the earlier view of counter-transference as a 'resistance' or 'blind-spot' in the analyst as it may obscure the importance of counter-transference by implying that it is something 'wrong'. This may encourage a 'phobic' attitude in the analyst towards his own emotional reactions and thus limit his understanding of the patient. He points out, in accord with views expressed by others (e.g. Winnicott, 1949), that the full use of the analyst's emotional response can be considered to be of particular importance in the treatment of patients with profound personality disorders and other very disturbed or psychotic patients. Hoffer has attempted to deal with some of the confusion connected with the term by distinguishing between the analyst's transference to his patient and his counter-transference, but idiosyncratically relates the analyst's transference to his humanity and appreciation of the patient's realistic needs,

66

and counter-transference to the analyst's intrapsychic reactions, including his limitations in comprehending the patient's material (1956).

A persistent theme in the psychoanalytic literature is that counter-transference phenomena are essential concomitants of psychoanalytic treatment. One of the clearest statements in this connection was made by Sharpe (1947) who says: 'To say that . . . an analyst will still have complexes, blind spots, limitations is only to say he remains a human being. When he ceases to be an ordinary human being he ceases to be a good analyst'. She adds:

'Counter-transference is often spoken of as if it implied a love-attitude. The counter-transference that is likely to cause trouble is the unconscious one on the analyst's side, whether it be an infantile negative or positive one or both in alternation. . . . We deceive ourselves if we think we have no counter-transference. It is its nature that matters.'

Similarly, A. Reich (1951) points out that 'counter-transference is a necessary prerequisite of analysis. If it does not exist, the necessary talent and interest is lacking, but it has to remain shadowy and in the background.' A similar view is put forward by Spitz (1956), and Little (1960b) who says 'without unconscious counter-transference there would be neither empathy nor analysis itself'. Money-Kyrle (1956) refers to empathy as the 'normal' counter-transference.

We can see that the concept of counter-transference has been broadened over the years, to include a number of different meanings, inevitably diminishing the precision with which it was originally used. In present usage the following main elements or meanings can be discerned. (Some of these have been listed by Little, 1951.)

1. 'Resistances' in the analyst due to the activation of inner conflicts in him. These disturb his understanding and conduct of the analysis, producing 'blind spots' (Freud, 1910a, 1912b).
2. The 'transferences' of the analyst to his patient. Here the patient becomes a present-day substitute for an important figure in the childhood of the analyst (e.g. A. Reich, 1951, 1960).
3. The disturbance of communication between analyst and

67

patient due to anxiety aroused in the analyst in the patient-analyst relationship (Mabel Blake Cohen, 1952).

4. Personality characteristics of the analyst which are reflected in his work and which may or may not lead to difficulties in his therapy (e.g. M. Balint and A. Balint, 1939); or the whole of the analyst's conscious and unconscious attitudes to his patients (e.g. Balint, 1949; Kemper, 1966).

5. Specific limitations in the psychoanalyst brought out *by particular patients*; also the specific reaction of the analyst to his patient's transference (e.g. Gitelson, 1952).

6. The 'appropriate' or 'normal' emotional response of the analyst to his patient. This can be an important therapeutic tool (Heimann, 1950, 1960; Little, 1951) and a basis for empathy and understanding (Heimann, 1950, 1960; Money-Kyrle, 1956).

Undoubtedly, the restriction of the clinical concept of counter-transference to the analyst's transference to his patient provides us with too narrow a definition, and one which is too closely tied to the particular meaning attributed to transference (Chaps. 4 and 5). The broadening of the concept to include all of the analyst's conscious or unconscious attitudes, and even all his personality traits, renders the term practically meaningless. On the other hand, it would seem appropriate to take into account the useful extension of the concept to include those aspects of the analyst's emotional responses to his patient which do not lead to 'resistances' or 'blind spots' in the analyst, but which may be employed by him, as far as he is able to become conscious of them, as a means of gaining insight (through an examination of his own mental reactions) into the meaning of the patient's communications and behaviour.

It would follow from this that the most useful view of counter-transference might be to take it as referring to the specific emotional responses aroused in the analyst by the specific qualities of his patient. This would exclude *general* features of the analyst's personality and internal psychological structure (which would colour or affect his work with all his patients) and would imply

1. That there are counter-transference responses in the analyst, and that these exist throughout the analysis.

2. That counter-transference can lead to difficulties in, or inappropriate handling of, the analysis. This will occur if and when the analyst fails to become aware of aspects of his counter-transference reactions to the patient, or fails to cope with them even if he is aware of them.

3. That constant scrutiny by the analyst of variations in his feelings and attitudes towards the patient can lead to increased insight into processes occurring in the patient.

Although it has not been stressed in the literature, we would suggest that the *professional attitude* of the therapist, which allows him to take a certain 'distance' from the patient and yet remain in touch with his own and the patient's feelings, is of the greatest service in the conduct of the analytic work. This professional stance (which is not at all the same as aloofness) is one of the factors which allows analysts to understand material in their patients which had not been adequately analysed in their own training analysis. It is also one of the factors, apart from intellectual insight, which enables certain therapists who have not been analysed, to do adequate psychotherapy, especially under the supervision of an analyst. It is probably in part responsible for the fact that some analysts can do better work than those who trained them. In putting forward this suggestion, we would emphasize that we do not underestimate the importance of the personal analysis in the training of psychoanalysts or the counter-transference resistances in the analyst due to the blind spots created by his own unresolved problems.

The concept of counter-transference can readily be extended outside psychoanalytic treatment, and awareness of the counter-transference can be regarded as a useful element in any doctor-patient or therapist-patient relationship. It follows that it can be of potential value for the clinician to monitor his reactions to his patients, and this can be extended to include the monitoring by the clinician of the reaction of other members of the staff of a therapeutic institution. For example, Main (1957) has described a group of patients who evoke a particular type of response in the medical and nursing staff of a psychiatric hospital. He suggests that this reaction, although it may be related to the internal problems and conflicts stimulated in the staff by such patients, is also the manifestation of an area of psychopathology in the patients themselves. The observation of counter-transference reactions may also be of diagnostic importance. For example, Hill (1956) has commented that a feeling of irritation in the doctor can suggest a diagnosis of hysteria in the patient.

Chapter 7

Resistance

While the *treatment alliance* (Chap. 3) and some aspects of *transference* (Chaps. 4 and 5) relate to tendencies within the patient which act to maintain the treatment relationship, the concept of *resistance* is concerned with elements and forces in the patient which oppose the treatment process. Although resistance is a clinical rather than a psychological concept (Chap. 1), originally described in connection with psychoanalytic treatment, it is one which can readily be extended, without substantial revision, to other clinical situations.

Resistance as a clinical concept emerged in Freud's discussion of his early attempts to elicit 'forgotten' memories from his hysterical patients. Before the development of the psychoanalytic technique of free association, when Freud was still employing hypnosis and the 'pressure' technique (Chap. 2), resistance was regarded as anything in the patient which opposed the physician's attempts to influence him. He saw these opposing tendencies as being the reflection, in the treatment situation, of the same forces which brought about and maintained the dissociation (repression) of painful memories from consciousness. He commented (1895):

> 'Thus a psychical force . . . had originally driven the pathogenic idea out of association and was now opposing its return to memory. The hysterical patient's "not knowing" was in fact a "not wanting to know" – a not wanting which might be to a greater or less extent conscious. The task of the therapist, therefore, lies in overcoming . . . this resistance to association.'

Resistance was regarded by Freud as being present in pathological states other than hysteria or obsessional neurosis (the

71

'defence neuroses'), e.g. in psychotic conditions. In describing his case of chronic paranoia (1896) he remarked that

'. . . in this case of paranoia, just as in the two other defence neuroses with which I was familiar, there must be unconscious thoughts and repressed memories which could be brought into consciousness in the same way as they were in those neuroses, by overcoming a certain resistance. . . . The only peculiarity was that the thoughts which arose . . . were for the most part heard inwardly or hallucinated by the patient, in the same way as her voices.'

In Freud's discussion of this case it becomes clear that he viewed the difference between the productions of the psychotic and those of the neurotic as being differences in form rather than content. What might emerge in the neurotic as a fantasy or in a dream, emerges in the psychotic patient as a belief (see the discussion of the psychotic transference in Chap. 5).

The motives for resistance were seen to be the threat of arousal of unpleasant ideas and affects. The ideas which had been repressed (and which resisted recollection) were regarded as characterized by being 'all of a distressing nature, calculated to arouse the affects of shame, of self-reproach and of physical pain, and the feeling of being harmed' (1895). The entry of psycho-analysis into what has been described as its second phase (Rapaport, 1959) and the recognition of the importance of inner impulses and wishes (in contrast to painful real experiences) in causing conflict and motivating defence did not bring about any fundamental change in the concept of resistance. Nevertheless resistance was now seen as being directed not only against the recall of distressing memories but also against the awareness of unacceptable impulses. In a paper on 'Freud's psycho-Analytic procedure' (1904), written by Freud himself, he states:

'The factor of resistance has become one of the corner-stones of his theory. The ideas which are normally pushed aside on every sort of excuse . . . are regarded by him as derivatives of the repressed psychical phenomena (thoughts and impulses), dis-torted owing to the resistance against their reproduction. . . . The greater the resistance, the greater is the distortion.'

In this formulation a new element can be seen. Resistance was no longer regarded as a complete suppression of unacceptable mental content, but as being responsible for the *distortion* of unconscious impulses and memories so that they appear *in disguise* in the free associations of the patient. In this context, resistance was seen to operate in exactly the same way as the 'censor' in dreaming (Freud, 1900), i.e. functioning to prevent unacceptable thoughts, feelings or wishes from becoming conscious.

The link between the clinical phenomenon of resistance and such 'distorting' or 'censoring' processes led naturally to the formulation that resistance is not something which appears from time to time during analysis, but is constantly present during that treatment. The patient 'must never lose sight of the fact that a treatment like ours proceeded to the accompaniment of a *constant resistance*' (1909c). In this paper Freud also commented on the satisfaction which patients receive from their sufferings, a point which he amplified elsewhere, and to which we will return later in this chapter, when we come to speak of the gratification obtained through suffering and through satisfaction of the need for punishment.

In Chapter 4 we commented on the importance which Freud attached to the relation between transference and resistance. The so-called 'transference-resistances' were regarded as the most powerful obstacles in the path of psychoanalytic treatment (1912a, 1940). Thoughts and feelings involving the person of the therapist may arise as a consequence of the patient's tendency to re-experience repressed earlier important attitudes, feelings and experiences instead of recalling them. These will tend to arise anew in the here-and-now of the analytic situation. The development of such transferences from past figures to the analyst may cause the most intense resistances to free association, for the patient's new feelings about the analyst may be felt to be extremely threatening.

'The patient who becomes dominated by a strong transference-resistance is flung out of his real relation to the doctor . . . feels at liberty then to disregard the fundamental rule of psycho-analysis which lays it down that whatever comes into one's head must be reported without criticizing it . . . forgets the intentions with which he started the treatment, and . . . regards with

73

indifference logical arguments and conclusions which only a short time before had made a great impression on him' (1912a).

Sources and Forms of Resistance

By this time, the major distinction made by Freud in regard to the sources of resistance in patients undergoing psychoanalysis was between *transference-resistance* and *repression-resistance*, the latter being the resistance, inherent in the psychological structure of the patient, to the awareness of painful or dangerous impulses and memories. While transference-resistances may disappear, and even be replaced by transference attachments which reinforce the treatment alliance, repression-resistances can be conceived of as an ever-present (though fluctuating) force which acts in opposition to the aims of treatment.

By 1926 Freud was in a position to distinguish between five major types and sources of resistance (1926a):

(1) *Repression-resistance*, which could be regarded as the clinical manifestation of the individual's need to defend himself against impulses, memories and feelings which, were they to emerge into consciousness, would bring about a painful state, or would threaten to cause such a state. The repression-resistance can also be seen as a reflection of the so-called 'primary gain' from the neurotic illness, inasmuch as neurotic symptoms can be regarded as being last-resort formations aimed at protecting the individual from conscious awareness of distressing and painful mental content. The process of free association during psychoanalysis creates a constant potential danger-situation for the patient, because of the invitation offered to the repressed by the process of free association, and this in turn promotes the repression-resistance. The closer the repressed material comes to consciousness, the greater the resistance, and it is the analyst's task to facilitate, through his interpretations, the emergence of such content into consciousness in a form which can be tolerated by the patient (Chap. 11).

(2) *Transference-resistance* which, although essentially similar to the repression-resistance, has the special quality that it both expresses, and reflects the struggle against, infantile impulses which have emerged, in direct or modified form, in relation

to the person of the analyst (Chap. 4). The analytic situation has reanimated, in the form of a current distortion of reality, material which had been repressed or had been dealt with in some other way (e.g. by its canalization into the neurotic symptom itself). This revival of the past in the psychoanalytic relationship leads to the transference-resistance. Here too, it is the analyst's task to assist the emergence of transference content into consciousness in a tolerable form by means of his interventions. Transference-resistances include the conscious withholding by the patient of thoughts about the analyst, as well as unconscious transference thoughts which are defended against.

(3) Resistance deriving from *the gain from illness* (secondary gain). Although in the first instance the symptom may be felt as a 'foreign body' and undesirable, a process of 'assimilation' of the symptom into the individual's psychological organization may, and often does occur. Freud put it thus: 'The ego now proceeds to behave as though it recognized that the symptom had come to stay and that the only thing to do was to accept the situation in good part and draw as much advantage from it as possible.' (1926a). Such secondary gains from symptoms are familiar in the form of the advantages and gratifications obtained from being ill and cared for or pitied by others, or in the gratification of aggressive and revengeful impulses towards those who are forced to share in the patient's suffering. Secondary gain may also accrue through the satisfaction of a patient's need for punishment, or of concealed masochistic trends. The grossest examples of gain from illness may be seen in patients with 'compensation neuroses', or those who remain ill because of the secondary gain from society, e.g. where 'welfare' payments exceed the wage that could be earned. The patient's reluctance to abandon these secondary advantages of illness, during the course of treatment, constitutes this particular form of resistance.

(4) *Id-resistance* due to the resistance of instinctual impulses to any change in their mode and form of expression. As Freud put it (1926b): 'And . . . as you can imagine, there are likely to be difficulties if an instinctual process which has been going along a particular path for whole decades is suddenly expected to take a new path that has just been made open for it'. This

form of resistance necessitates what Freud called 'working through' for its elimination (Chap. 10).*

(5) '*Superego-resistance*', or the resistance stemming from the patient's sense of guilt or his need for punishment. Freud regarded the 'superego-resistance' as being the most difficult for the analyst to discern and to deal with. It reflects the operation of an 'unconscious sense of guilt' (1923), and accounts for the apparently paradoxical reaction of the patient to any step in the analytic work which represents the fulfilment of one or other impulse which he has defended against because of the promptings of his own conscience. Thus a patient who has strong guilt feelings related, for example, to the wish to be the most-loved son and to triumph over his siblings, may react with resistance to any change which threatens to bring about a situation in which he can become more successful than his rivals. Or a patient who has intense unconscious feelings of guilt about his particular sexual wishes may react with strong resistance following the freeing of such wishes through the analytic process. 'Superego-resistance' can be exemplified by the patient who allows himself to have a thought which arouses guilt, represses this thought, and comes to the session with an uneasy feeling which is eventually identified as a feeling of guilt which has made him resistant to the work of analysis. The most intense form of such superego-resistance can be seen in the so-called 'negative therapeutic reaction', to be discussed in Chap. 8.

Freud saw the clinical phenomena of resistance as being intimately (though not exclusively) related to the whole range of the patient's mechanisms of defence, not only to the mechanism of repression, although he often used the term 'repression' as a synonym for defence in general. These mechanisms are developed and utilized to deal with situations of danger (in particular, the

*This type of resistance in treatment can be regarded as a consequence of the more general psychological resistance to giving up acquired habits and modes of functioning – a resistance to 'unlearning'. An aspect of the concept of 'working through' would be the process of learning new patterns of functioning and learning to inhibit the older, more firmly established patterns. This is a process which is regarded as constituting an important part of the analytic work. The 'id-resistance' has also been referred to in psychoanalytic writings as 'sluggishness' or 'adhesiveness' of the libido.

dangers which would arise if unconscious sexual or aggressive wishes were to be allowed free and direct expression in consciousness or in behaviour), and include such defence mechanisms as projection, undoing, intellectualization, rationalization, identification with the aggressor, reaction formation, etc. '. . . the defensive mechanisms directed against former danger recur in the treatment as *resistances* against recovery. It follows from this that the ego treats recovery itself as a new danger' (Freud, 1937a).

Freud had made a number of references to the relation between the form of the resistance shown by the patient and the nature of the underlying defensive organization. For example, he had described particular types of distortion of free association which were thought to be characteristic of obsessional neurotics (1909c). But while the types of resistance were felt to be indicative of aspects of the patient's psychopathology (1926a), they were, in the main, regarded by Freud as essentially obstacles to the work of analysis.

In 1936 Anna Freud, in her book *The Ego and the Mechanisms of Defence*, emphasized the extent to which the resistances can provide information on the patient's mental functioning. Resistances, insofar as they reflect the type of conflict and the defences used, were an object of analytic study in themselves. Analysis of resistances could be seen as essentially the analysis of those aspects of the patient's defences which entered into and contributed to the pathological outcome of his conflicts. 'Defence-analysis', via the analysis of resistances, has come to play an increasingly important part in psychoanalytic technique (Hartmann, 1951; Glover, 1955; A. Freud, 1965).

In a number of important publications, Wilhelm Reich (1928, 1929, 1933) had demonstrated that certain patients had developed fixed character traits which were the outcome of past defensive processes, and which showed themselves both in the personality and in the psychoanalytic process as characteristic 'fixed' attitudes. Reich referred to these as the 'armour-plating of character' (*Charakterpanzerung*), but while he maintained that resistances due to such 'fixed' personality characteristics should initially be the primary focus of the psychoanalytic work, Anna Freud maintained that they should be placed in the foreground only when no trace of a current conflict could be detected (A. Freud, 1936).

In 1939, Helene Deutsch proposed a three-fold classification of forms of resistance into (i) the intellectual or 'intellectualizing' resistances, (ii) the transference-resistances, and (iii) those resistances which emerge as a consequence of the patient's need to defend himself against the recollecting of childhood material. She discussed the first group *in extenso*, commenting that patients who show the intellectual resistances attempt to replace analytic *experiencing* with intellectual *understanding*. Such resistances may be found in highly intellectual individuals, in obsessional neurotics and in patients 'with blocked or disturbed affects, who, having repressed the affective side of their life, have retained the intellectual side as the sole means of expressing their . . . personality'.

In spite of the close link between resistance and defence, it has been repeatedly emphasized that resistance is not synonymous with defence (Gerö, 1951; Loewenstein, 1954; Lorand, 1958). Whereas the patient's defences are an integral part of his psychological structure, resistance represents the patient's attempts to protect himself against the threats to his psychological equilibrium posed by the analytic procedure. As Greenson (1967) puts it: 'The resistances defend the *status quo* of the patient's neurosis. The resistances oppose the analyst, the analytic work, and the patient's reasonable ego'.

An examination of the psychoanalytic literature since Freud indicates that the *concept* of resistance in psychoanalysis has remained essentially unchanged. However, the *forms* which resistance can take have been described in detail, and there is little doubt that the sensitivity to subtle signs of resistance has come to be regarded as an increasingly important part of the psychoanalyst's repertoire of technical skills. It might be of some use to follow the descriptive differentiation made by Glover (1955) between the 'obvious' or 'crass' resistances on the one hand, and the 'unobtrusive' resistances on the other. The 'crass' resistances include breaking-off treatment, lateness, missing appointments, silences, circumlocution, automatic rejection or misinterpretation of everything the analyst says, assumed stupidity, a persistent mood of abstraction and falling asleep.*

* Some forms of resistance, e.g. falling asleep and silence, may, at certain points in the analysis, be regarded not only as resistance but as non-verbal forms of expression of repressed wishes, fantasies or memories (Ferenczi, 1914; Khan, 1963).

The less obtrusive resistances are hidden beneath an apparent compliance with the requirements of the analytic situation. They may show themselves in the form of agreement with everything the analyst says, in the bringing of material (e.g. dreams) in which the patient believes the analyst to have a special interest, and in many other forms. As Glover remarks: 'On the whole, the characteristic of these unobtrusive resistances is just that they are not explosive, do not break through or disrupt the superficies of the analytic situation, but rather infiltrate the situation, exude through it, or, to vary the expression, move with the stream rather than against it, snagwise'. Fenichel (1945a) has distinguished between 'acute' resistances as opposed to the more hidden forms, the latter showing themselves mainly in the lack of change in the patient, even though the psychoanalytic work appears to be proceeding without hindrance. Because of the difficulties involved in the classification of the *forms* of resistance, all attempts at such classification appear to be of the nature of an academic exercise. The range of forms which resistances can take is probably infinite, and it would appear to be more fruitful to investigate the different *sources* of resistances, as these are probably much more limited in number, and indicate something of the motivation for the particular resistance, and its function at a particular time.

All authors now tend to agree that it is an important part of the psychoanalytic process for the analyst to make the patient aware of his resistances, to attempt to get the patient to view them as obstacles which have to be understood and overcome. They also agree that this can be a far from easy task, for the patient will often make every attempt to justify or rationalize his resistance, to view it as appropriate in the circumstances. The threat which the analytic work may constitute to the particular equilibrium which the patient has established may be so great that he may even manifest his resistance through a 'flight into health', and justify the cessation of treatment by the fact that his symptoms have, for the time being at least, disappeared. Here the fear of what might occur as a consequence of the analysis would appear to be so great as to outweigh the primary and secondary gains from the symptoms. The mechanisms whereby the 'flight into health' can be accomplished are, in our view, insufficiently understood, but it seems more likely that this process can take place when the secondary gains from illness have played an important part in maintaining the patient's symptoms, after the primary gain from the symptoms has receded or disappeared. The 'flight into health' should be distinguished from the denial of symptoms, which may be part of the patient's justification for stopping treatment when the resistances aroused outweigh the treatment alliance.

As far as the sources of resistance are concerned, those outlined by Freud (1926a) remain central in the theory of psychoanalytic technique. However, the list may be extended and modified in the light of later contributions. It should be emphasized that the various categories listed below overlap greatly.

(1) Resistances due to the threat posed by the analytic procedure and its aims to the particular adaptations made by the patient. In this context the concept of adaptation is used as referring to the individual's adaptation to forces arising both from the external world and from within himself (Sandler and Joffe, 1969). The repression-resistance can be included here, being a specific case of what might be termed 'defence-resistance', for defences other than repression can give rise to resistance. The mechanisms of defence can, in turn, be regarded as mechanisms of adaptation, and are essential for normal functioning as well as being involved in pathogenic processes (A. Freud, 1936).

(2) Transference-resistances, essentially as described by Freud (see page 74).

(3) Resistance deriving from secondary gains, as described by Freud (see page 75).

(4) Superego-resistance, as described by Freud (see page 76).

(5) Resistance arising from faulty procedures and inappropriate technical measures adopted by the psychoanalyst. Such resistances may be dealt with during the normal course of the analysis, if their source is realized and acknowledged by both analyst and patient. If this does not occur, these resistances may lead to a breakdown of treatment or its continuation on a spurious basis (Glover, 1955; Greenson, 1967).

(6) Resistances due to the fact that changes in the patient brought about by the analysis may lead to real difficulties in the patient's relationships with important persons in his environment. Thus a masochistic and subservient spouse

may offer a resistance to insight and change because such a change would threaten the marriage.

(7) Resistances prompted by the danger of cure and the loss of the analyst which this might entail. Many patients remain in analysis because of concealed gratifications obtained from the procedure and the analytic relationship, particularly where the patient has come to depend on the person of the analyst as an important figure in his life. Thus a patient may unconsciously re-experience the analyst as a protecting or nurturing parent, and the resistance to cure may reflect a fear of giving up the relationship. Such patients may get worse when termination of treatment is considered, but this is not the same as the negative therapeutic reaction which is a form of 'superego-resistance' (see page 75 and Chap. 8).

(8) Resistances due to the threat of the analytic work to the patient's self-esteem (Abraham, 1919). This is particularly important in those patients in whom the arousal of *shame* is a major motive for defensive activity. Such patients may have difficulties in tolerating the infantile aspects of themselves which emerge during the course of treatment because they regard these aspects as shameful.

(9) Resistance to the giving up of past adaptive solutions (including neurotic symptoms) due to the fact that such solutions need to be 'unlearned' or extinguished. This process of extinction takes time, and is an integral part of the process of working through (Chap. 10). While this includes the so-called 'id-resistance', it also encompasses sources of resistance to change in modes of functioning of the more organized and controlling aspects of the personality (i.e. of the ego and superego).

(10) Character resistances, of the sort described by Wilhelm Reich (1928, 1929, 1933), due to the 'fixed' nature of character traits which may persist after the original conflicts which brought them into being have diminished or disappeared, which are acceptable to the patient because they do not give rise to distress.

While the last two forms of resistance are obviously related, and may even be considered to be forms of 'secondary gain', the basis for the resistance is different from what is usually conceived of as 'secondary gain'. It has been suggested that an adaptive solution, be it a neurotic symptom, a character trait, or some other method of functioning can be reinforced (and thus offer a resistance to change once the original 'primary gain' has disappeared) by the fact that its predictability and availability as a pattern of functioning creates an increment in the individual's feelings of safety (Sandler, 1960a). This has been described by Sandler and Joffe (1968) in relation to the persistence of the psychological 'structures' which are regarded as patterning aspects of behaviour. They remark:

'Some structures may evolve in order to solve ongoing conflict. But they may persist and be utilized in order to maintain safety feeling even though the original impulses· which entered into their formation are no longer operative in the same way. It is likely that the latter structures are [those] most amenable to change through behaviour therapy. Thus a neurotic symptom (and the structures which subserve it) may be directed towards solving, for example, an ongoing conflict between an instinctual wish and internal (superego) standards of the individual. But it may equally function at a later date as a method of producing safety feeling, and if other methods of providing safety feeling are available then a different and more comfortable solution may be created and utilized, and the employment of the older symptom-structure inhibited. . . . All systems and techniques of psychotherapy (including behaviour therapy) abound with potential alternative safety-giving solutions which can be adopted by the patient.'

While resistance was originally conceived of in terms of the patient's resistances to recollection and to free association, it is clear that the concept was soon extended to include all the obstacles to the aims and procedures of treatment which arise from within the patient. In psychoanalysis and psychoanalytic psychotherapy resistances are overcome by means of the analyst's interpretations and other interventions (Chap. 11). The form and context of the resistance has come to be seen as a useful source of information to the therapist. Such a view of resistance enables the concept to be extended from psychoanalysis to all forms of treatment, and we can see the manifestations of resistance even in ordinary medical practice, in the form of forgotten appointments, misunderstandings of the doctor's instructions, rationalizations for breaking off treatment, and the like. Different methods of treatment may stimulate different sources of resistance, and this may account for the fact that one method may succeed with a patient when another would not. Indeed, some methods of treatment may owe their success to the fact that they by-pass certain sources of resistance, but it must be equally true that others may fail because no provision has been made for the adequate handling of the resistances which may arise. Even in all these different situations, the resistance may itself be a source of useful information.

Chapter 8

The Negative Therapeutic Reaction

The clinical concept of the *negative therapeutic reaction* has been included in this book for a number of reasons. It is a concept of particular importance in the history of psychoanalysis, for it represents the clinical phenomenon chosen by Freud (1923) to illustrate the workings of an 'unconscious sense of guilt' and to indicate the existence of what he conceived of as a special mental agency – the *superego*. Moreover, it is a concept widely used in clinical psychoanalysis, although little has been written on the subject since Freud's original formulation. Unlike such concepts as *transference* (Chaps. 4 and 5) and *acting out* (Chap. 9), it has not been extensively applied outside clinical psychoanalysis. This may be regarded as surprising in view of the fact that it would seem to be readily capable of application without alteration to a wide variety of clinical situations.

The phenomenon of the negative therapeutic reaction in psychoanalytic treatment was first described and explained by Freud as follows (1923):

'There are certain people who behave in a quite peculiar fashion during the work of analysis. When one speaks hopefully to them or expresses satisfaction with the progress of the treatment they show signs of discontent and their condition invariably becomes worse. One begins by regarding this as defiance and as an attempt to prove their superiority to the physician, but later one comes to take a deeper and juster view. One becomes convinced, not only that such people cannot endure any praise or appreciation, but that they react inversely to the progress of the treatment. Every partial solution that ought to result, and in other people does result, in an improvement or a temporary suspension of symptoms produces in them for the time being an exacerbation of their illness; they get worse during the treatment instead of getting better.'

Freud linked this with the operation of what he conceived of as an unconscious sense of guilt, due to the operation of the patient's conscience (an aspect of the superego).* In these cases the illness can be regarded, in part at least, as serving the function of allaying or reducing the patient's sense of guilt. His symptoms may represent a need for punishment or suffering, an attempt to appease an unduly harsh and critical conscience. It follows that recovery, or the promise of recovery, represents a particular type of threat to these patients, viz. the danger of experiencing acute and perhaps unbearable feelings of guilt. It is suggested that in some way the state of being free from symptoms must in such patients represent the fulfilment of unconscious childhood wishes, the gratification of which is felt to be internally forbidden.

Shortly afterwards, in writing on masochism (1924), Freud added that the 'unconscious sense of guilt', which could lead to the negative therapeutic reaction, might in some cases be reinforced by a concealed unconscious masochistic tendency. This would lead to a further gain from the suffering due to the illness, and present an increased resistance to recovery. He suggests that 'The suffering entailed by neuroses is precisely the factor that makes them valuable to the masochistic trend', and added that

'contrary to all theory and expectation . . . a neurosis which has defied every therapeutic effort may vanish if the subject becomes involved in the misery of an unhappy marriage, or loses all his money, or develops a dangerous organic disease. In such instances, one form of suffering has been replaced by another. . . .'

It may be of some interest that Freud suggested in this paper that the idea of an unconscious sense of guilt is one which is difficult to explain to patients and which is in fact psychologically

* See Sandler (1960b) and Sandler, Holder and Meers (1963) for a discussion of the relation of conscience to the superego.

incorrect.* He remarked that the idea of a 'need for punishment' aptly covers the observed state of affairs.

Freud thus used 'negative therapeutic reaction' as (i) a *description* of a particular clinical phenomenon, i.e. the worsening of the patient's condition following some encouraging experience (e.g. the analyst's expression of satisfaction with the progress of the analytic work or the patient's own realization that progress had been made through the elucidation of some problem). This occurs when we might normally expect him to experience relief. (ii) An *explanation* of the clinical phenomenon in terms of a psychological mechanism, i.e. a reaction, which takes the form of getting or feeling worse instead of better, aimed at reducing the guilt feelings evoked by improvement. In people who show this reaction, improvement can be thought of as representing the gratification of an internally forbidden wish, and is consequently experienced as a threat.

The negative therapeutic reaction was seen by Freud as being a characteristic of certain types of patient in analysis, and it is of interest that he had, some years earlier, described essentially the same mechanism in an entirely different context. In 1916 he had included, in the description of a number of different character types, 'those wrecked by success'. Beginning from the comment that neurosis originates in the frustration of an instinctual wish, he goes on to comment:

'So much the more surprising, and indeed bewildering, must it appear when as a doctor one makes the discovery that people occasionally fall ill precisely when a deeply-rooted and long-cherished wish has come to fulfilment. It seems then as though they were not able to tolerate their happiness; for there can be no question that there is a causal connection between their success and their falling ill.'

Freud illustrated his thesis by reference to the case of a woman who had lived happily with her lover for many years, seeming only to need legalization of their union to achieve complete happiness.

---

* Freud maintained that feelings cannot appropriately be described as 'unconscious' (1923, 1924) but believed that the same factors which produce conscious feelings of guilt can operate outside conscious awareness, and that the concept of an 'unconscious sense of guilt' is useful in spite of philosophical and semantic objections to it.

When, finally, she and her lover were married, she broke down completely, developing an incurable paranoid illness. Freud also cites the case of a teacher who had for many years cherished the wish to succeed the master who had initiated him into his studies. When he was in fact chosen as the successor, he developed feelings of doubt and unworthiness, and succumbed to a depressive illness which lasted for some years.*

'Analytic work', said Freud, 'has no difficulty in showing us that it is forces of conscience which forbid the subject to gain the long hoped-for advantage from the fortunate change in reality' (1916).

Apart from an increasing recognition of the clinical importance of the negative therapeutic reaction, the psychoanalytic literature on the specific topic is relatively sparse. Wilhelm Reich (1934) suggested that the occurrence of the negative therapeutic reaction was due to faulty analytic technique, particularly the failure to analyse the negative transference, and a paper by Feigenbaum (1934) describes a relevant clinical fragment. However, two papers published shortly afterwards attempt to extend Freud's original concept to include a number of different mechanisms (Rivière, 1936; Horney, 1936).

In 1936 Joan Rivière pointed out that the negative therapeutic reaction as described by Freud did not mean that the patient was always unanalysable. The patient who reacts in this way does not always break off treatment, and changes may be brought about in the patient through appropriate analytic work. Rivière went on to suggest that 'Freud's title for this reaction, however, is not actually very specific; a negative therapeutic reaction would just as well describe the case of any patient who does not benefit from a treatment'. Rivière appears to have treated the concept more broadly than did Freud, and included a number of types of severe resistance to analysis (in particular, refractory cases). In common with a number of later authors (e.g. Rosenfeld, 1968) she included certain forms of resistance in which the patient either explicitly or implicitly rejects the analyst's interpretations. Much of Rivière's discussion relates to what we have described as resistance due to the threat of the analytic work to the patient's self-esteem and resistances due to 'fixed' character traits (Chap. 7). Other aspects relate to the

*Freud quoted Lady Macbeth as well as Rebecca West in Ibsen's *Rosmersholm* as examples.

absence of an adequate treatment alliance in certain types of patient (Chap. 3).

In contrast to Rivière, another important technical paper by Karen Horney (1936) begins with the formulation that the negative therapeutic reaction is not, indiscriminately, every deterioration of the patient's condition. She suggests that only those instances ought to be included in which one might reasonably have expected the patient to feel relief. She goes on to say that in many cases of negative therapeutic reaction 'the patient very often actually feels this relief distinctly, and then after a short while reacts as described, e.g. with an increase in symptoms, discouragement, a wish to break off treatment, etc. A definite sequence of reactions appears, in principle, to be present. First, the patient experiences a definite relief, followed by a shrinking back from the prospect of improvement, discouragement, doubts (about himself or the analyst), hopelessness, wishes to break off, and makes remarks like "I am too old to change." '

Horney suggested that the negative therapeutic reaction is embedded in persons with a particular type of 'masochistic' personality structure. In such persons the effect of a 'good' interpretation by the analyst (in the sense that the interpretation is felt by the patient to be correct) may be considered to be of five kinds. These are not always present nor equally strong, but may exist in different combinations.

(1) Such patients receive a 'good' interpretation as a stimulus to compete with the analyst. The patient is resentful of what he feels to be the analyst's superiority. Horney considers competitiveness and rivalry to be above average in such patients, who are extremely ambitious. Fused with their ambition is an inordinate amount of hostility. They often express their hostility and their sense of defeat by belittling the analyst and attempting to defeat him. The patient's reaction in this case is not to the content of the interpretation but to the skill shown by the analyst.

(2) The interpretation may also be regarded as a blow to the patient's self-esteem when it reveals to him that he is not perfect and has 'ordinary' anxieties. He feels reproached and may show a negative reaction in an attempt to turn the tables by reproaching the analyst.

(3) The interpretation is followed by a feeling of relief, however fleeting, and the patient reacts as if the solution means a move towards recovery and success. This reaction would appear to embody both a fear of success and a fear of failure. While on the one hand the patient feels that if he attains success he will incur the same sort of envy and rage that he feels towards the success of others, on the other he fears that if he makes a move towards ambitious aims and fails, others will crush him as he would like to crush them. Such patients recoil from all aims involving competition and impose a constant inhibiting or checking process on themselves.

(4) The interpretation is felt as an unjust accusation, and the patient constantly feels as if the analysis is a trial. The interpretation reinforces existing feelings of self-condemnation, and the patient reacts by accusations directed against the analyst.

(5) The patient feels the interpretation to be a rebuff, and takes the uncovering of his own difficulties as an expression of dislike or disdain on the part of the analyst. This type of reaction is related to a strong need for affection and an equally strong sensitivity to rejection.

These types of reaction are elaborated on by Horney, and we have mentioned them here at some length because of their obvious clinical importance. However, in spite of her initial precise description of the negative therapeutic reaction, Horney (like Rivière) includes other 'negative' responses based upon different underlying psychological processes. While these are important from the point of view of the treatment of patients with 'narcissistic' and 'masochistic' personality structures, they differ in quality from the negative therapeutic reaction as described by Freud. The patient who shows this reaction *deteriorates* when he might be expected to improve, and this is quite different from the patient who *resents* a 'correct' interpretation, or who shows some form of aggressive 'contrariness'.

Clinical evidence of the existence of a negative therapeutic reaction in patients who have strong guilt feelings and a 'need for punishment' may sometimes be gained from the paradoxical reaction of such patients to interpretations which are felt by them to be an attack, criticism or punishment. This is shown in a case of a very masochistic patient described by Sandler (1959).

'Much of her silence and difficulty in association was meant to provoke me to anger and being relatively inexperienced at the time, I occasionally . . . betrayed my irritation with her either by my comments or in the tone of my voice. Whenever this happened, she would relax and the following session would be a "good" one; she would associate well and new material would emerge. This I understood at the time as being a result of having involuntarily satisfied her "need for punishment". . . .'

The psychoanalytic writings on or relevant to this topic (e.g. Feigenbaum, 1934; Rivière, 1936; Horney, 1936; Ivimey, 1948; Eidelberg, 1948; Lewin, 1950; Cesio, 1956, 1958, 1960a, 1960b; Greenbaum, 1956; Brenner, 1959; Salzman, 1960; Arkin, 1960; Olinick, 1964; Rosenfeld, 1968) have, it appears to us, added little to our knowledge and understanding of this mechanism provided that we retain the specific features of the reaction described by Freud. Much of the published literature deals with more general types of resistance and 'negativistic' attitudes, or links the negative therapeutic reaction with masochism in general. These papers contribute to the further understanding of negativism and masochism but, as we have said, do not throw much light on the specific characteristics of the negative therapeutic reaction, but rather tend to blur its specificity. It seems worthwhile to retain the term 'negative therapeutic reaction' for the phenomenon and the mechanism as originally described by Freud and linked by him with the need for the patient to protect himself against guilt feelings associated with the experience or possibility of success or improvement. However, the prognosis in analysis for patients who show this reaction is thought to be far better than in the early days of psychoanalysis, due to improvements in the technical handling of guilt reactions via the analysis of the transference. Inasmuch as this mechanism, like others, develops in the child in relation to important figures of childhood, so the understanding of the repetition of these relationships in the patient's transference to the analyst can allow for the development of different ways of reacting and for mitigating the effects of a harsh conscience.

A notably useful review paper by Olinick (1964) reviews the many misconceptions which exist among analysts as to the nature of the negative therapeutic reaction. He too is concerned about the tendency to blur the term and comments 'One occasionally still hears the term employed as a designation for any and all worsenings of the patient's condition during treatment. This gratuitously nullifies the meticulous clinical observations of previous writers.' Olinick speaks of 'counterfeit' negative therapeutic reactions to describe the effect of faulty technique when an interpretation of an unconscious wish is given before the patient has been adequately prepared for it. Instead of experiencing relief, the premature interpretation makes the patient feel worse, but this is not a negative therapeutic reaction in the sense described by Freud.

Olinick goes on to consider the negative therapeutic reaction as a special case of negativism. He traces the origins of a negativistic attitude to the early years of life, and links it with situations which foster feelings of resentful aggressiveness and contrariness in the child.

The occurrence of the negative therapeutic reaction in patients who are prone to depression is a theme which has been referred to in the literature from 1936 onwards (Rivière, 1936; Horney, 1936; Gerö, 1936; Lewin, 1950, 1961). It seems likely that, for some patients, success represents, paradoxically, a move away from, or a loss of, an 'ideal' state of the self connected with certain harsh demands of the patient's conscience. It is probably the loss of this 'ideal' which is associated with the development of a depressive reaction (Joffe and Sandler, 1965). A further, though less direct link between the negative therapeutic reaction and depression can be traced, in our own clinical experience, to the attempts made by certain patients, who show a tendency to the negative therapeutic reaction, to develop symptoms which are aimed at warding off or preventing the development of a depressive state. The development of such symptoms has been described in relation to psychogenic pain (Joffe and Sandler, 1967).

Inasmuch as we can regard the propensity for negative therapeutic reactions to reside in the character of the individual, rather than being a function of the psychoanalytic treatment situation, these apparently paradoxical reactions to the threat of recovery or success can be regarded as occurring equally in other clinical situations. Thus it is to be expected that they can be detected as responses in certain individuals to progress (or to expressions of

91

satisfaction by the therapist) in treatment of any sort. It would also follow that the previous histories of these individuals would indicate similar 'negative' reactions to experiences of success and achievement.

It should be pointed out that there are a number of other reasons for a patient relapsing in situations in which improvement has occurred. These may be quite distinct from the negative therapeutic reaction as described by Freud. For example, at the time of the termination of treatment a temporary return of symptoms may occur. This is observed in other treatment situations, as when discharge from hospital or suggestion of cessation of out-patient attendance is discussed with the patient. Some relapses may be thought of in such terms as unresolved dependency of the patient upon the person of the doctor. Similarly, relapses may also represent attempts to deal with fears of breakdown after cessation of treatment which are now coped with by falling ill again before the end of treatment.

The negative therapeutic reaction appears to be a clear-cut clinical phenomenon, and its occurrence does not necessarily indicate faulty technique or inappropriate intervention on the part of the therapist. However, we would emphasize again that there appears to be a multitude of causes for treatment failing or being ineffective, which do not constitute the negative therapeutic reaction.

Knowledge of the mechanism, and of the prognostic significance of the particular type of character structure in which the negative therapeutic reaction may occur, has a wide clinical application. Thus, for example, it can lead the clinician to be careful about suggesting to depressed patients who show strong guilt feelings and a pattern of reacting which corresponds to the negative therapeutic reaction, that they should 'take a holiday'. The guilt engendered by this may lead to severe pain and depression, even to the extent of precipitating suicide.

In conclusion, we can summarize by saying that the term 'negative therapeutic reaction' is used in the following ways:

(1) As a description of the situation in which worsening follows an awareness by the patient or expression by the therapist of improvement.

(2) As an explanation of this clinical phenomenon, in which the

reappearance of symptoms are ascribed to the operation of guilt engendered by the atmosphere of encouragement, optimism, or approval.

(3) The phrase has been extended in the literature to describe a character reaction of 'negativism' or contrariness that becomes manifested in a clinical setting as opposition to, or failure to accept benefit from, treatment. Such patients may, of course, improve during treatment, but they do not admit to it. While this is of clinical importance, it does not seem to us to be a useful extension of Freud's concept, and may diminish its utility.

(4) It has been used, in our view incorrectly, to include many other forms of resistance to the process of psychoanalytic treatment.

Chapter 9

Acting Out

Of all the clinical concepts considered in this book, *acting out* has probably suffered the greatest extension and change of meaning since it was first introduced by Freud (?Freud, 1905b; Holder, 1970). Blos comments that:

> '...the concept of acting out is overburdened with references and meanings. The rather clear-cut definition of thirty years ago when acting out during analysis was considered a legitimate and ana-lysable form of resistance has by now been expanded to accom-modate delinquent behaviour and all kinds of . . . pathology and impulsive actions. This expansion of the concept has reached a conceptual breaking point. I feel . . . [as if I am] groping my way through the underbrush of an overgrown concept eager to find a clearing which would permit a wider view' (1966).

The term now tends to be used (by psychoanalysts and others) to include a whole range of impulsive, anti-social or dangerous actions, often without regard to the contexts in which such actions arise. It is sometimes used in a pejorative sense to denote disap-proval of actions of patients or even colleagues. Examination of the relevant recent literature (e.g. Abt and Weissman, 1965) shows the great variety of current usages, the only common denominator appearing to be the assumption that the particular action referred to as 'acting out' has unconscious determinants.

Part of the present confusion surrounding the concept derives from the translation of the term originally used by Freud. In 1901, in *The Psychopathology of Everyday Life*, he had made use of the colloquial German term *handeln* (to act) in his description of 'faulty' acts or parapraxes which could be understood to have an unconscious significance. In 1905, however, in his description of the 'Dora' case he made use of the less colloquial word *agieren* (also meaning 'to act', but with a slightly more emphatic connotation) in a particular technical sense. *Agieren* was translated as 'acting out' and it is probable that the choice of this latter term, and in particular the inclusion of the preposition 'out', has contributed to some of the changes in meaning of the concept in the English and American literature.*

Freud's patient 'Dora' broke off treatment after some three months, and he subsequently attributed this abrupt termination to his failure to notice the patient's transference on to him of feelings towards an important figure of the past (Herr K.). He wrote:

'In this way the transference took me unawares, and, because of the unknown quantity in me which reminded Dora of Herr K., she took her revenge on me as she wanted to take her revenge on him, and deserted me as she believed herself to have been deceived and deserted by him. Thus she *acted out* an essential part of her recollections and phantasies instead of producing it in the treatment' (1905b).

Here acting out was related to transference and resistance, and it was also seen as a substitute for remembering. She did not recollect the past and report it in her free associations, but instead enacted the memory.

Freud's most extensive discussion of the concept is to be found in his technical paper on 'Remembering, repeating and working-through' (1914a). Here acting out is related quite strictly to the clinical psychoanalytic treatment situation. As in the 'Dora' case, it is used to refer to actions which the patient produces as substitutes for memories.

' . . . the patient does not *remember* anything of what he has forgotten and repressed, but *acts* it out. He reproduces it not as

---

* Thus Bellak says 'Freud first mentioned acting out in *The Psychopathology of Everyday Life*' (but here Bellak confuses *handeln* and *agieren*). He goes on to describe practically every type of clinically significant action as one or other variety of 'acting out' (1965). The implicit equation of acting (*handeln*) and acting out (*agieren*) is also made by Greenacre (1950) and Rexford (1966).

a memory but as an action; he *repeats* it, without, of course, knowing that he is repeating it. . . . For instance, the patient does not say that he remembers that he used to be defiant and critical towards his parents' authority; instead, he behaves that way to the doctor.'

Freud goes on to refer to acting out as a *way of remembering* which makes its appearance in the analysis. He draws attention to the fact that transference, too, can be regarded as a 'piece of repetition', and that transference and acting out are at one when the patient repeats the past in a way which involves the person of the physician (as when the patient falls in love with the analyst). However, he also relates acting out to resistance. 'The greater the resistance, the more extensively will acting out (repetition) replace remembering . . . if, as the analysis proceeds, the transference becomes hostile or unduly intense and therefore in need of repression, remembering at once gives way to acting out.'

Freud distinguishes between acting out *within* the analytic situation and acting out *outside* the analysis. Both forms are regarded as a consequence of the analytic work and the treatment situation. Within analysis, the transference provides the vehicle for acting out, and this may be the only way in which repressed memories may initially find their way to the surface. Acting out outside the analysis carries with it potential dangers to the treatment and to the patient, but it is often impossible to prevent such acting out, nor indeed is such interference always desirable. Freud comments that although one tries to protect the patient from injuries consequent on carrying out his impulses by obtaining a promise that he take no important decisions affecting his life during treatment

'At the same time one willingly leaves untouched as much of the patient's personal freedom as is compatible with these restrictions, nor does one hinder him from carrying out unimportant intentions, even if they are foolish; one does not forget that it is in fact only through his own experience and mishaps that a person learns sense. There are also people whom one cannot restrain from plunging into some quite undesirable project during the treatment, and who only afterwards become ready for, and accessible to, analysis. Occasionally, too, it is bound to happen that the untamed instincts assert themselves before there is time to put the reins of the transference on them, or that the bonds which attach the patient to the treatment are broken by him in a repetitive action' (1914a).*

Freud's views on acting out remained essentially unaltered in his subsequent discussions of the subject (1920, 1939, 1940), and it is clear that he consistently regarded acting out as a *clinical* psychoanalytic concept related quite specifically to psychoanalytic treatment (cf. also A. Freud, 1936).

Departures from Freud's original usage began to occur fairly early in the subsequent psychoanalytic literature, and a number of factors appear to be responsible for this. Some of these are listed below.

(1) A comment made by Freud, taken out of context, has been used to broaden the concept substantially. In considering what it is that the patient repeats under conditions of resistance, Freud remarked: 'We may now ask what it is that he in fact repeats or acts out. The answer is that he repeats everything that has already made its way from the sources of the repressed into his manifest personality – his inhibitions and unserviceable attitudes and his pathological character traits. He also repeats all his symptoms in the course of the treatment' (1914a). This should not be taken to imply that repetition and acting out are synonymous, even though acting out is a form of repetition. Nor does Freud's statement remove acting out from its *clinical* context.

(2) The choice of acting *out* as the translation of *agieren* has resulted in certain authors restricting the concept to acting out *outside* the analytic treatment situation. This has led to the coining of the term 'acting in' for some aspects of what Freud referred to as acting out within the analysis (Zeligs, 1957; Rosen, 1965; Eidelberg, 1968).

(3) The tendency to broaden psychoanalytic theory into a general psychology (Hartmann, 1939, 1944, 1964) has led to the reformulation of a number of clinical concepts in more general psychological terms. This tendency was, of course, encouraged by Freud's repeated references to the fact that the phenomena

* As analyses now take longer than in the past, the request to patients to refrain from making major decisions (e.g. marriage) during the course of the analysis has tended to be modified or abandoned.

which can be observed in psychoanalytic treatment can also be observed outside it. A consequence of attempts to generalize clinical concepts is that they may lose something of their clinical precision. This has been discussed in relation to transference (Chap. 4), and the same considerations appear to apply to acting out.

(4) The concept of acting out was derived in the context of the psychoanalytic method applied to adult patients who were predominantly neurotic, and who were regarded as being capable of adhering to the basic technical rule of free association. With the application of psychoanalysis to the treatment of patients with severe personality disorders, to psychotics, adolescents and children, new technical problems arose, and this resulted in a widening of the concept. Because of similarities between the impulsive aspects of the behaviour of patients in the above-mentioned groups and the acting out of the neurotic patient (under the pressure of the analysis) the temptation to label all impulsive behaviour as 'acting out' was very strong (A. Freud, 1968).

(5) Acting out was regarded by Freud as a particular manifestation of resistance which could have undesirable consequences for the patient or for the progress of his analysis. Because of this it appears to have been a natural step for his colleagues and followers to apply it more to behaviour which was 'undesirable' in a general sense than to other forms of behaviour Carried to its extreme, socially or morally undesirable behaviour (in patients and others) tended by some to be labelled 'acting out'.

Acting out has been discussed by Fenichel with reference both to treatment-related phenomena and to impulsive tendencies lodged in the personality and pathology of the individual (1945b). He linked the tendency to impulsive action with difficulties in the first year of life, these giving rise to a tendency to react to frustrations with violence. He also suggested that traumatic experiences in childhood may lead to repeated attempts to master, through activity, what was once passively and traumatically experienced. It is of interest that Fenichel distinguished more sharply than Freud had done between transference and acting out, suggesting that the tendency to act out was a function of the particular individual concerned, and can consequently be considered in a wider context than that of psychoanalytic treatment. Individuals who show a proclivity for acting out will tend to act out whether they are in analysis or not. They have

'in common an insufficient differentiation between the present and the past, an unwillingness to learn, a readiness to substitute certain rigid reactive patterns for adequate responses to certain stimuli. But these reactive patterns . . . are not necessarily real actions – sometimes they consist in mere emotional attitudes; and we rather call it "transference" if the attitude concerns definite persons, and "acting out" if something has to be done regardless towards whom' (1945b).

Fenichel's main point – that certain persons show a greater tendency to express their unconscious impulses in action than others – is an interesting one, but his retention of the term 'acting out' for such impulsive actions widens the link which previously existed between acting out and transference-resistance. In discussing acting out in this way, he was in fact discussing a different topic, i.e. the character of those individuals who tend to *enact* in an impulsive fashion.

Greenacre has also discussed acting out as a habitual phenomenon which creates special problems of therapeutic management. She defines acting out as

'a special form of remembering, in which the old memory is re-enacted in a more or less organized and often only slightly disguised form. It is not a clearly conscious visual or verbal recollection, nor is there any awareness that the special activity is motivated by memory. His behaviour seems to the subject to be plausible and appropriate' (1950).

This last characteristic of acting out has been emphasized in much of the subsequent literature (e.g. Greenson, 1967). Greenacre also considers the developmental determinants of habitual forms of acting out, and to those enumerated by Fenichel (1945b) she adds 'a special emphasis on visual sensitization producing a bent for dramatization . . . and a largely unconscious belief in the magic of action'. Greenacre's formulations suggest that the later tendency to habitual acting out is chiefly the result of certain disturbances in the first two years of life. The link between acting out and

99

preverbal experiences has been emphasized in much of the subsequent psychoanalytic literature, especially by the followers of Melanie Klein (e.g. Bion, 1962; Rosenfeld, 1965b; Meltzer, 1967).

The tendency to use the term to refer, more or less indiscriminately, to actions of all sorts has increased in recent years, and we find a whole volume entitled *Acting Out* (Abt and Weissman, 1965) devoted to a discussion of such diverse behavioural disturbances as drug addiction, alcoholism, psychosomatic illness, obesity, homosexuality, learning inhibitions and the like, all regarded as special forms of acting out. In the foreword to this book, Bellak remarks:

'Even in its narrower definition, acting out is of great social importance. The character disorder, be it as a carrier of emotional contagion within a small family group, or as a demagogue of national scale, is a serious problem. The delinquent, the adult criminal, the drug addict, the ordinary psychotic, as well as the political lunatic, are problems of great social import which demand solutions. We need to know how to prevent the development of such bad actors, understand them well enough to control them therapeutically or socially, and we need to know right now most urgently how to predict who is likely to act out and when.'

Similarly, Helene Deutsch has widened the concept from a clinical one to one of general psychology.

'To some extent, we are all actors-out, because nobody is free of regressive trends, repressed strivings, burdens of more or less conscious fantasies, etc. Artists are able to create in acting out their work of art; neurotics of every type and degree are using their symptoms to act out; hysterics in conversion symptoms, and often very dramatic twilight states; obsessionals in their ceremonies; psychotics in hallucinations and delusions; delinquents in their asocial behaviour' (1966).

Such extension of the concept would appear to rob it entirely of its original meaning, and it is perhaps unfortunate that some such term as 'enactment' was not used in the literature to distinguish the general tendency to impulsive or irrational action from acting out linked with the treatment process. Moreover, such an extension appears to add to the pejorative connotation of the term.

100

In the more recent literature, a reaction to the indiscriminate use of the term can be discerned, and some psychoanalytic writers have begun to advocate a return to the narrower concept and, in particular, to emphasize its application to the enactment of unconsciously determined urges during the course of treatment (e.g. Limentani, 1966; Greenson, 1967; A. Freud, 1968; Rangell, 1968). With this development, there has also been a move away from looking upon acting out as undesirable and towards its evaluation as a source of information and its significance as a special form of communication or expression.* In this respect, the assessment of the concept of acting out as a clinical phenomenon has undergone a similar change to that which occurred in the case of transference (Chap. 4) and counter-transference (Chap. 6), both of which were initially regarded as obstacles to treatment, but which were later seen as valuable sources of information. With this, there has also been a move away from regarding acting out exclusively as a form of resistance, particularly against transference (Greenson, 1967; Rangell, 1968), to evaluating it as a possible first indication of new material emerging from unconscious sources. Limentani (1966), for instance, quotes the example of the patient who calls at the analyst's consulting room at the usual time, having overlooked the fact that there was no session because of a national holiday. He suggests that there may be little evidence of resistance in such behaviour, and it can be taken as a useful source of analytic material. Balint (1968) has made a similar point in regard to the analysis of patients who have a 'basic fault' in their personalities.

To sum up, it can be said that the concept of acting out has been used in psychoanalysis in two main senses.

(1) To describe certain behavioural phenomena which arise during the course of an analysis, and which are a consequence of that treatment. The concept refers to mental contents (wishes, memories, etc.) which are pushing their way towards the surface as a consequence of their revival in the analytic

* A point which had, in fact, been made by Fenichel who commented (1941) '. . . we must think of so-called "acting out" from the therapeutic point of view. In individuals who do not indulge in it generally, acting out is a welcome sign that in the analysis something has happened which we can and must utilize in finding out the unconscious processes behind it.'

treatment situation, these contents being enacted rather than remembered. If they involve the person of the analyst, their enactment has been referred to as 'acting out in the transference', but acting out includes other treatment-related and treatment-inspired forms of enactment. In its original sense, acting out can occur either within the treatment setting or outside it. The term 'acting in', introduced more recently, would refer simply to acting out within the treatment situation.

(2) To describe habitual modes of action and behaviour which are a consequence of existing personality and pathology, and which are related to the type of individual rather than to the treatment process. Perhaps the most lucid statement regarding such individuals is that given by Hartmann (1944): 'There is . . . a large number of people in whom active social conduct represents not a rational action but an "acting out", which is more or less neurotic, in relation to social reality. In this "acting out" they repeat infantile situations and seek to utilize their social conduct to resolve intrapsychic conflicts. A strong reliance on reality can also be used to overcome fear. It can, but it does not need to, have the character of a symptom. It also depends on the peculiarities of the social milieu, what conflicts and anxiety tensions are overcome by the social behaviour. On the other hand, sometimes a modification of the social structure which limits this activity . . . leads to a reappearance of those conflicts which were temporarily overcome and serves to precipitate a neurosis.'

The application of the concept of acting out to behaviour arising in contexts other than that of psychoanalytic treatment poses certain difficulties. These do not arise if we use the concept in its widest sense, i.e. as relating to individual personality tendencies, for these exist apart from the treatment situation. In the narrower and technical sense, however, a problem arises if we adhere to the view that acting out is a substitute for remembering. Other forms of treatment, with different goals and using different methods, may not involve or stimulate the recall of the patient's childhood past. Nevertheless the concept would, it seems, be capable of extension if it were linked with those situations (therapeutic and otherwise) in which an intense relationship fosters a tendency to a revival of earlier, especially infantile, states and impulses. Enactments of these earlier states can occur, and these could, in our view, be legitimately referred to as acting out. An example of such acting out might be the case of a patient receiving behaviour therapy who develops unconscious hostile feelings towards his therapist as a consequence of his dependence on the therapist, and who may enact these towards someone else. Similarly, an inpatient may deal with irrational guilt feelings which have developed, in the regression fostered by the hospital situation, towards his doctor by provoking reproval or 'punishment' from the hospital authorities. The awareness and understanding by the doctor of acting out tendencies occurring within a treatment situation of any sort can be of value, it would seem, not only in the handling of the patient but also in gaining clues with regard to his psychopathology. Acting out is, of course, not only confined to the patient group. Irrational actions towards patients resulting from the doctor's counter-transference could probably also be designated as acting out on the part of the doctor. And, insofar as intra-staff relationships may foster infantile attitudes, the irrational behaviour which may arise in response, say, to the death or retirement of a key figure in the institution, may lead to behaviour which could be designated as acting out. There is no doubt, however, that such an extension of the concept does imply a certain change in meaning from the original psychoanalytic usage. This will render it somewhat less precise in its application.

Chapter 10

Interpretations, Other Interventions and Insight

Previous chapters have concentrated on concepts which relate to the communications brought by the patient, and to the factors in both patient and therapist which either facilitate or hinder the free flow and understanding of these communications. In the chapter on *working through* (Chap. 11), we shall discuss those interventions of the analyst which aim at bringing about enduring changes in the patient, and the need for continual elaboration and reinforcement of the analyst's interventions. The term 'interpretation' is often used in a general sense to refer to such interventions (at least, to the extent that they are verbal) and here we will examine the concept in some detail.

Interpretation and other interventions
Interpretation occupies a special place in the literature on psychoanalytic technique. Thus Bibring (1954) has remarked that '*Interpretation* is the supreme agent in the hierarchy of therapeutic principles characteristic of analysis . . .'. The central role of interpretation is equally stressed by M. Gill (1954) who asserts that 'Psychoanalysis is that technique which, employed by a neutral analyst, results in the development of a regressive transference neurosis and the ultimate resolution of this neurosis by techniques of interpretation alone.'

Because the psychoanalytic technique is predominantly a *verbal* one, and because the psychoanalytic training has become so specialized, it is perhaps natural that a certain mystique has

104

become attached to the analyst's 'interpretations'.* Menninger (1958) has commented:

'Interpretation is a rather presumptuous term, loosely applied by (some) analysts to every voluntary verbal participation made by the analyst in the psychoanalytic treatment process. I dislike the word because it gives young analysts the wrong idea about their main function. They need to be reminded that they are not oracles, not wizards, not linguists, not detectives, not great wise men who, like Joseph and Daniel, "interpret" dreams – but quiet observers, listeners, and occasionally commentators. Their participation in a two-party process is predominantly passive . . . their *occasional* active participation is better called intervention. It may or may not "interpret" something. It may or may not be an interruption. But whenever the analyst speaks he contributes to a process. . . .'

As we have described, Freud, in his early writings (1895), wrote of the recovery of 'forgotten' memories by his patients. At that time he restricted his own verbal interventions in the therapeutic situation to those required to induce the necessary free expression of the patient's thoughts. He attempted to avoid direct suggestion of the sort which had characterized the hypnotic methods from which the psychoanalytic technique derived. His comments and suggestions were directed only towards *facilitating* the patient's production of verbal material, in the belief that the stream of associations would eventually lead to the recall, more or less spontaneously, of emotionally charged memories surrounding important and significant events of the patient's past. In the early days of psychoanalysis the emotional abreaction which accompanied such recall was regarded as the essential therapeutic agent, for the patient's symptoms were thought to be brought about by the persistence of 'dammed-up' affects. Freud gradually formed the view that the hysterical patient's symptoms also symbolized, unbeknown to the patient, aspects of the assumed traumatic event and the thoughts and feelings connected with that (now forgotten) event. By 1897 Freud had given up the traumatogenic theory of hysteria and was devoting himself to a searching examination of processes of symbolic representation, especially as they

* Some analysts even adopt a special tone of voice when delivering interpretations.

occurred in dreams. As is well-known, his study of his own and his patients' dreams was published in *The Interpretation of Dreams* (1900).

Freud's first references to interpretation are to dream interpretation. The concept referred, in this connection, to the analyst's own understanding and reconstruction of the hidden sources and meaning of the dream ('latent content'). This was arrived at by an examination of the free associations of the patient to the conscious memory of the dream itself ('manifest content'). In the early years of psychoanalysis the analyst conveyed and explained his interpretation to the patient, but this was a relatively didactic communication to the patient of the interpretation arrived at by the analyst.

By the time Freud came to write his papers on psychoanalytic technique (1911b, 1912a, 1912b, 1913a, 1914a, 1915a) he commented that there had been changes in the manner of presentation of the psychoanalyst's understanding of the patient's productions. The analyst's interpretation of the patient's dreams and free associations was not to be freely imparted, but might be withheld until resistances appeared. Freud now expressed his 'condemnation of any line of behaviour which would lead us to give the patient a translation of his symptoms as soon as we have guessed it ourselves . . .'. (1913a). From this time onwards Freud more or less consistently distinguished between the interpretation and the *communication* of the interpretation. Thus he wrote (1926b):

'When you have found the right interpretation, another task lies ahead. You must wait for the right moment at which you can communicate your interpretation to the patient with some prospect of success. . . . You will be making a bad mistake if . . . you throw your interpretations at the patient's head as soon as you have found them.'

In 1937 Freud differentiated between interpretations and 'constructions' in analysis. ' "Interpretation" applies to something that one does to some single element of the material, such as an association or a parapraxis.* But it is a "construction" when one

* This particular definition has a strange ring, coming relatively late in Freud's writings. The definition, as given here, has not been maintained in the subsequent literature. No emphasis is placed now on the 'single' element as the subject of interpretation.

lays before the subject of the analysis a piece of his early history that he has forgotten' (1937b). A construction (now usually called a 'reconstruction') represents a 'preliminary labour' which facilitates the emergence of memories of the past or their repetition in the transference.

While, early on, interpretation was regarded as a process occurring in the mind of the analyst, no great confusion could arise if the term was also applied to what the analyst said to the patient, for (apart from restrictions imposed by the need for 'analytic tact') the content of the two was the same. With the increasing realization that resistances and defences had also to be pointed out to the patient, more emphasis began to be placed on the *form* in which the analyst gave his comments and explanations to the patient. This has led to a use of the term 'interpretation' in the psychoanalytic literature after Freud which emphasizes what the analyst says to the patient rather than being restricted to the analyst's understanding of the patient's productions. The term is now regularly employed to describe one or other aspect of the analyst's comments. The 'art of interpretation' demanded of the analyst has come to mean the art of making a successful verbal intervention of a particular sort rather than the art of understanding the unconscious meaning of the patient's material. Thus Fenichel (1945a) refers to interpretation as 'helping something unconscious to become conscious by naming it at the moment it is striving to break through'.

It would seem that the change in the concept was an inevitable result of the introduction of the structural theory by Freud (1923, 1926a), and the move away from the previous 'topographical' conception (Chap. 1). More and more stress came to be laid, in the area of psychoanalytic technique, on formulating interpretations which were acceptable to the patient, or which would be particularly effective at a given time. Stress was laid on *what* the analyst chooses to relay to the patient, *when* he chooses to do it, and on the *form* in which he does it (W. Reich, 1928; Anna Freud, 1936; Fenichel, 1941, 1945a; Hartmann, 1939, 1951; Kris, 1951; Loewenstein, 1951; Greenson, 1967).

It should be noted that from 1897 to 1923 the patient's free associations were regarded as being surface derivatives of unconscious wishes and impulses 'forcing their way to the surface from the depths'. The problem of interpretation was seen predominantly as one of understanding 'deeper' unconscious material from the analysis of conscious productions. The structural view-point emphasized the role of the organized part of the personality (the ego) in finding compromises between instinctual urges (the id), dictates of conscience and of ideals (the superego) and external reality. Interpretations were seen as being addressed to the ego of the patient, and its strengths and weaknesses had to be taken into account. The analyst was forced to consider the *effect* of what he wanted to say. This is exemplified by Fenichel's anecdote of the analyst who unsuccessfully interpreted, for weeks on end, the patient's wish to kill him. While the analyst's understanding of the patient's unconscious wish appeared to be correct, what the analyst said to the patient did not appear to be so.

> 'Such an interpretation in that sort of situation *augments* the anxiety and with it the ego's defence, instead of diminishing it. The correct interpretation would have been [according to Fenichel]: "You cannot talk because you are afraid that thoughts and impulses might come to you which would be directed against me" ' (1941).*

The situation at present appears to be that the term 'inter-pretation' is used both as a synonym for nearly all the analyst's verbal (and even occasionally non-verbal) interventions on the one hand, and as *a particular variety* of verbal intervention on the other.

There has been relatively little attempt in the literature to distinguish, at a descriptive level, between the various components of the analyst's verbal interventions. Loewenstein (1951) considers that those comments of the analyst which 'create conditions with-out which the analytic procedure would be impossible' are not interpretations, but rather comments which aim at freeing the patient's associations (e.g. 'those which induce the patient to follow the fundamental rule, the purpose of which is to loosen the barrier or censorship existing normally between conscious and pre-conscious processes . . .'). Interpretations proper are verbal interventions which produce 'those dynamic changes which we

---

* There are analysts who still regard their task as that of continuously interpreting deeply unconscious material to the patient, and who apparently take the view 'the deeper the better'.

call insight'. He thus excludes instructions and explanations from the concept of interpretation, considering the latter to be a term 'applied to those explanations, given to patients by the analyst, which add to their knowledge about themselves. Such knowledge is drawn by the analyst from elements contained and expressed in the patient's own thoughts, feelings, words and behaviour.'*

Loewenstein also draws attention to interventions which could be called 'preparations for interpretation', as, for example, the analyst's pointing out similar patterns in experiences thought by the patient to be quite unconnected.

Eissler (1953) points out that some interventions (e.g. commands to phobic patients) are not part of the 'basic model of the psychoanalytic technique'. They constitute what he calls 'parameters of technique'. In the same paper, Eissler adds that certain verbal interventions other than interpretations are also essential to the 'basic model of psychoanalytic technique'. These include those instructions thought to be appropriate for the particular patient (e.g. about the basic rule of free association) and questions aimed at elucidating the material. He takes the view that 'the question as a type of communication is a basic and therefore indispensable tool of analysis, and one essentially different from interpretation'. Olinick (1954) provides a useful discussion of the role of questioning in psychoanalytic technique.

Greenson has dissected some of the verbal components of analytic techniques (1967). He considers that 'The term analysing is a shorthand expression which refers to . . . [certain] . . . insight-furthering techniques.' Among these he includes:

Confrontation. This is regarded as a process of drawing the patient's attention to a particular phenomenon, making it explicit, and getting him to recognize something which he has been avoiding and which will have to be further understood.
Clarification. While this may follow confrontation, and blend with

* Loewenstein introduces a certain problem here in defining an interpretation on the basis of the effect it produces, i.e. dynamic changes leading to insight. We can readily conceive of interpretations which are correct but not effective, and conversely of interpretations which are incorrect but effective (Glover, 1931). It would seem that defining an interpretation by its aim rather than by its effect might produce greater conceptual clarity.

it, it represents more the process of bringing the psychological phenomena with which the patient has been confronted (and which he is now more willing to consider) into sharp focus. It involves the 'digging out' of significant details which have to be separated from extraneous matter.

Interpretation. This means 'to make conscious the unconscious meaning, source, history, mode or cause of a given psychic event. This usually requires more than a single intervention.'

In addition to these three (often interwoven) procedures, *working through* is added by Greenson as the fourth component of the procedure of analysis (Chap. 11).

To sum up, the term *interpretation* has been used in the psychoanalytic literature to mean the following:

(1) The analyst's inferences and conclusions regarding the unconscious meaning and significance of the patient's communications and behaviour.
(2) The communication by the analyst of his inferences and conclusions to the patient.
(3) All comments made by the analyst. This is a common colloquial usage of the term.
(4) Verbal interventions which are specifically aimed at bringing about 'dynamic change' through the medium of insight.

Some authors have differentiated the following from interpretation:

(1) Instructions given to the patient about analytic procedure in order to create and maintain the analytic setting.
(2) Constructions (or reconstructions) of aspects of the patient's early life and experiences, derived from material brought or enacted during the analysis.
(3) Questions aimed at eliciting and elucidating material.
(4) Preparations for interpretation (for example, the demonstration of recurring patterns in the patient's life).
(5) Confrontations, as described by Greenson (1967).
(6) Clarifications, as described by Greenson (1967).

The degree of arbitrariness in many of these distinctions is striking. It is fairly generally accepted in the psychoanalytic literature that no interpretation can ever be complete, and perhaps the most practical use of the concept would be to include within it all comments and other verbal interventions which have the aim of immediately making the patient aware of some aspect of his psychological functioning of which he was not previously conscious. This would *include* much of what has been referred to as 'preparations for interpretation', confrontations, clarifications, reconstructions, etc. It would *exclude* the normal and inevitable verbal social interchanges and instructions as to analytic procedure. While these may nonetheless have an effect on the patient (e.g. the reassurance gained through the arrangement of regular appointments), we would suggest that an interpretation should be seen from the point of view of the analyst's intention of providing insight rather than on the basis of the effect of the analyst's remarks on the patient. Rycroft has elegantly described what could, from this point of view, be regarded as the central element in interpretation. He says (1958):

'The analyst invites the patient to talk to him, listens, and from time to time talks himself. When he talks, he talks neither to himself nor about himself *qua* himself, but to the patient about the patient. His purpose in doing so is to enlarge the patient's self-awareness by drawing his attention to certain ideas and feelings which the patient has not explicitly communicated but which are nonetheless part of and relevant to his present psychological state. These ideas, which the analyst is able to observe and formulate because they are implicit in what the patient has said or in the way in which he has said it, have either been unconscious, or, if they have been conscious, it has been without any awareness of their present and immediate relevance. . . . In other words, the analyst seeks to widen the patient's endopsychic perceptual field by informing him of details and relations within the total configuration of his present mental activity which for defensive reasons he is unable to perceive or communicate himself.'

Attempts to narrow the concept of interpretation have a secondary effect on interpretative technique, particularly if certain interpretations are thought to be the only 'good' interventions. Such an effect has been evident in regard to the value put on transference interpretations which, because they have been regarded by some analysts as the only 'proper' form of interpretation, have become the only interpretations given by some analysts. Consequently, all interpretations may be forced into a 'transference' mould (see Chaps. 4 and 5, and the comment on 'mutative' interpretations made below).

The content of interpretations has received a considerable degree of attention in the literature, particularly from the point of view of the relative effectiveness of different types of interpretation. In what follows we shall list some of the varieties of interpretation which have been described.

Some Other 'Types' of Interpretation

Content interpretation is an expression used to denote the 'translation' of the manifest or surface material into what the psychoanalyst understands to be its deeper meaning, usually with particular emphasis on childhood sexual and aggressive wishes and fantasies. This was the predominant type of interpretation given in the first decades of psychoanalysis. Such interpretations are concerned only with the meaning (unconscious content) of what was thought to have been repressed rather than with the conflict and struggle which has kept the memories and fantasies unconscious. Together with *symbolic* interpretations, which are the translation of symbolic meanings as they appear in dreams, slips of the tongue, etc., content interpretations are popularly regarded as constituting the bulk of the psychoanalyst's activity, a misconception which dates from Freud's early work.

Defence interpretation is a particular form of the analysis of resistances (Chap. 7). Such interpretations are aimed at showing the patient the mechanisms and manoeuvres which he uses to deal with the painful feelings involved in a particular conflict and, if possible, the origins of these operations. Defence interpretations are thought to be an indispensable complement to content interpretations, as the latter are thought to be insufficient unless the patient is also shown the way in which he copes with infantile impulses in himself. Anna Freud (1936) remarks that

'a technique which confined itself too exclusively to translating symbols would be in danger of bringing to light material which

112

consisted, also too exclusively, of id-contents. . . . One might seek to justify such a technique by saying that there was really no need for it to take the circuitous route by way of the ego. . . . Nevertheless, its results would still be incomplete.'

Defence interpretations are also believed to be of special importance in bringing about a modification in the neurotic patient, as his psychopathology is considered to be rooted, in part, in his particular defensive organization, i.e. in his particular methods of coping with conflict. Changes in this organization are considered to be an essential part of the therapeutic process (Chap. 7).

The idea that some interpretations are more effective than others is embodied in the concept of the *mutative* interpretation. Strachey (1934) suggested that the crucial changes in the patient brought about by interpretation are those which affect his super-ego. Interpretations which have this effect are considered to be 'mutative', and in order to be effective must be concerned with processes occurring in the immediate 'here-and-now' of the analytic situation (as, in Strachey's view, only interpretations of such immediate processes, especially transference processes, have sufficient urgency and impact to bring about fundamental change). This idea has contributed, as has been mentioned earlier, to the view that only *transference* interpretations (Chaps. 4 and 5) should be given by the analyst, as these are the only interpretations which can be effective (mutative). This does not appear to have been Strachey's belief, and does not accord with the practice of the majority of analysts, who make use of *extra-transference* interpretations (or *non-transference* interpretations) as well.

Direct interpretations are those given as an immediate response to the patient's material, without waiting for further associations or clarification (e.g. Rosen, 1953). They are often a form of symbolic interpretation.

The Presumptive Mode of Action of Interpretations
The relation of therapeutic success to the making of 'correct' interpretations has occupied a number of authors. For example, Glover (1931) has suggested that inexact, inaccurate and incomplete interpretations may still result, in certain circumstances, in therapeutic progress. He regards this effect as coming about

through the provision for the patient of an alternative system or organization which can act as a 'new substitute product' (in place of the previous symptom) which 'is now accepted by the patient's ego'.

Susan Isaacs (1939), in discussing the process of interpretation, took the view that the good analyst, by virtue of his training, used interpretations as scientific hypotheses concerning the patient's functioning. She says that

'this becoming aware of the deeper meaning of the patient's material is sometimes described as an intuition. I prefer to avoid this term because of its mystical connotation. The process of understanding may be largely unconscious but it is not mystical. It is better described as a *perception*. We perceive the unconscious meaning of the patient's words and conduct as an objective process. Our ability to see it depends . . . on a wealth of processes in ourselves, partly conscious and partly unconscious. But it is an objective perception of what is in the patient, and it is based upon actual data.'

The emphasis on the 'objective perception of objective data' has been disputed by Rycroft (1958), who suggests that what Freud did was not to explain a phenomenon

'causally, but to understand it and give it meaning, and the procedure he engaged in was not the scientific one of elucidating causes but the semantic one of making sense of it. It can indeed be argued that much of Freud's work was really semantic and that he made a revolutionary discovery in semantics, viz. that neurotic symptoms are meaningful disguised communications, but that, owing to his scientific training and allegiance, he formulated his findings in the conceptual framework of the physical sciences.'

Isaacs' contention that the analyst's perception of unconscious meaning is an objective process is highly disputable, to say the least. But, on the other hand, the contrast between 'scientific' and 'semantic' as made by Rycroft is also open to question.

An intermediate view appears to be that of Kris (1956), who refers to

114

'the well-known fact that the reconstruction of childhood events may well be, and I believe regularly is, concerned with some thought processes and feelings which did not necessarily "exist" at the time the "event" took place. They may either never have reached consciousness or may have emerged at a later time, during the "chain of events" to which the original experience became attached. Through reconstructive interpretations they tend to become part of the selected set of experiences constituting the biographical picture which in favourable cases emerges in the course of analytic therapy.'

Balint (1968) has pointed out that the particular analytic language and frame of reference of a psychoanalyst must inevitably determine the way a patient comes to understand himself. From this point of view it would appear that therapeutic change as a consequence of analysis depends, to a large degree, on the provision of a structured and organized conceptual and affective framework within which the patient can effectively place himself and his subjective experience of himself and others (cf. Novey, 1968).

The concept of interpretation is obviously not limited to the psychoanalytic treatment setting or to various forms of psychodynamic psychotherapy. The verbalization by a general practitioner of a patient's unformulated fears about his health can be conceptualized as an interpretation, as it has the intention of conveying new insight by presenting to the patient some aspect of his feelings and behaviour of which he was not previously aware. It does not follow, of course, that the type of interpretation appropriate in one setting is always appropriate in others.

Insight

The concept of 'insight' is one which is widely used in psychoanalysis, in the systems of psychotherapy derived from it, and in dynamic psychiatry in general. The term is generally used as if its meaning is readily apparent, but close study soon reveals that the term is anything but clear. As Zilboorg (1952) has put it: 'Among the unclarities which are of utmost clinical importance and which cause utmost confusion is the term insight. It came from nowhere, so to speak. No one knows who employed it first, and in what sense.'

115

There appears to be a complex relationship between the psychoanalytic and psychiatric meanings of the term. In general psychiatry 'insight' was introduced to indicate the patient's 'knowledge that the symptoms of his illness are abnormalities or morbid phenomena' (Hinsie and Campbell, 1970). This is the sense in which the term has been used in psychiatry since the early years of this century, and remains in use with this particular meaning. Jung, speaking of psychotic patients who have severe intellectual and emotional impairment, remarks that they can have 'signs of more or less extensive insight into the illness' (1907). Following Kraepelin (1906), Bleuler (1911) and Jaspers (1913), the 'absence of insight' is principally associated with psychotic mental states. However, although the word 'insight' has, particularly in the last twenty years, been extended from psychiatry to psychoanalysis, the specific psychiatric meaning has been lost in the extension to psychoanalysis. It is worth noting that the *early* use of the term in psychoanalysis was not a specialized technical one. The term does not appear in the index of the Standard Edition of the *Complete Psychological Works of Freud,* although it has been used in a non-technical sense at various points in the text. It would seem that a relatively colloquial word in both German and English (the German is *Einsicht*) was elevated, at some point in the history of psychoanalysis, to the status of a technical concept.* Nonetheless, the concept, in the more technical forms in which it is now used in psychoanalysis, appears to be firmly rooted in Freud's formulations regarding the processes of change which lead to 'cure'.

In 1893 Breuer and Freud had written:

'We found, to our great surprise, at first, that *each individual hysterical symptom immediately and permanently disappeared when*

---

* The Oxford English Dictionary points out that the 'original notion appears to have been "internal sight", i.e. with the eyes of the mind or understanding'. Among the definitions given are 'Internal sight, mental vision or perception, discernment . . .' and 'The fact of penetrating with the eyes of the understanding into the inner character or nature of things; a glimpse or view beneath the surface . . .' It is of interest that present, more or less colloquial, usage seems to have been affected by the psychoanalytical technical concept, so that its meaning at times approaches a sense which, paradoxically, the Oxford English Dictionary describes as obsolete, i.e. 'understanding, intelligence, wisdom'.

we had succeeded in bringing clearly to light the memory of the event by which it was provoked and in arousing its accompanying affect, and when the patient had described that event in the greatest possible detail and had put the affect into words. Recollection without affect almost invariably produces no results' (1895).

A similar point was made by Freud who commented of the patient that

'If we can succeed in eliciting a really vivid memory in him, and if he sees things before him with all their original actuality, we shall observe that he is completely dominated by some affect. And if we then compel him to put this affect into words, we shall find that, at the same time as he is producing this violent affect, the phenomenon of his pains emerges very markedly once again and that thenceforward the symptom, in its chronic character, disappears' (1895).

The element of 'cognitive' knowledge – 'the memory of the event' – was stressed by Freud in the first phase of psychoanalysis *in the context of emotional release.* The idea of recovery through affect discharge in the form of abreaction was related to the notion of a specific traumatic event being the pathogenic agent in such conditions as hysteria. The necessity for an emotional accompaniment to the recovery of repressed memories is very close to what many psychoanalysts nowadays regard as 'emotional insight'.

With the change in Freud's view of pathogenesis due to the shift of emphasis from an external traumatic event to the vicissitudes of the instinctual drives (in 1897), and his increasing interest in the interpretation of dreams (1900), the emotional element seemed to recede. The analyst's insight was now more or less equated with his understanding of the meaning of the patient's productions, and it was this understanding which he communicated to the patient, often making use of explanations and intellectual arguments. The gradual realization of the importance of the need to analyse the transference and transference resistances led to an awareness once more of the importance of the emotional context in which the patient's understanding was embedded. As Freud put it:

'It is true that in the earliest days of analytic technique we took an intellectualist view of the situation. We set a high value on the patient's knowledge of what he had forgotten, and in this we made hardly any distinction between our knowledge of it and his. . . . It was a severe disappointment when the expected success was not forthcoming' (1913a).

The term does not appear to have been used in the title of a psychoanalytic paper until that by French on 'Insight and Distortion in Dreams' in 1939. French quite explicitly took over the term from the Gestalt psychologist W. Köhler (1925). Köhler had described how the perception by an experimental animal of the way to solve a problem may occur suddenly as an 'insight'. French regarded insight in psychoanalysis as a similar phenomenon, i.e. as 'a "practical grasp" of the conflict situation'. Such insight was not regarded by French as a therapeutic agent *per se* but as a precondition for the further 'problem-solving' that could lead to cure.

The major problem in the psychoanalytic literature following Freud appears to lie in the need to define the qualities which distinguish 'true' or 'emotional' insight on the one hand and purely intellectual insight on the other. It is generally believed by psychoanalysts that the distinction is one which can be made and that it is of crucial importance from the point of view of analytic technique. The bare intellectual knowledge of the psychoanalytic view of the sources of disturbance is manifestly ineffective (as otherwise a patient might be cured by giving him a textbook of psychoanalysis to read). It would seem that, from the point of view of psychoanalytic therapy, some form of emotional experience is an essential accompaniment of what is regarded as effective insight. However, the definition of what constitutes 'true', 'emotional' or 'effective' insight has posed problems of definition with which many writers have struggled (e.g. Kubie, 1950; Zilboorg, 1952; Reid and Finesinger, 1952; Martin, 1952; Richfield, 1954; Silverberg, 1955; Kris, 1956; Valenstein, 1962; Myerson, 1960, 1963, 1965; Segal, 1962; Pressman, 1969a, 1969). One of the difficulties inherent in the problem of finding a suitable definition of effective psychoanalytic insight has been the temptation to succumb to a tautology, viz. if insight is ineffective in producing change, it is not 'true' insight. *Ergo*, insight which brings about change is effective.

118

If we are to avoid these difficulties, it would appear to be necessary to divorce the concept of emotional insight from the concept of 'cure', for it does not follow that such insight is necessarily followed by progressive and therapeutic changes in the patient. Reid and Finesinger (1952) and Richfield (1954) have attempted to apply philosophical analysis in their efforts to clarify the problem. The former authors make use of the term 'dynamic insight' as the efficacious variety, quoting Kubie's (1950) statement that 'insight begins to have therapeutic effect only when it leads to an appreciation of the relationship between varied experiences and the unconscious conflicts, out of which arises both the neurotic components of the personality and the neurotic symptoms themselves'. Reid and Finesinger themselves attempt to distinguish between 'neutral' and 'emotional' insight. The former is meant 'to imply that neither of the terms in the relation whose significance is grasped by the act of insight is an emotion, nor does the act of insight mediate or release at the time an emotional response in the person who has the insight'. In 'emotional' insight 'the emotion is a part of the subject-matter into which the patient has insight, or, more precisely, it is a term in the relation whose significance is grasped through insight'. Alternatively, insight may be regarded as 'emotional' or 'dynamically effective' if 'it makes the patient conscious of a fact, which itself may or may not be an emotion, that *releases* or *sets off* an emotional response'. This appears to be the closest definition of insight from a psychoanalytic point of view which is not necessarily tied to the criterion of 'correctness' or therapeutic change.

It appears to us that the notion of 'correct' insight leads to a great many difficulties. At the same time, the concept of 'effective' insight may result in a tautological argument. Perhaps the most useful approach to the problem is to differentiate 'intellectual' insight from those forms of insight which either release emotions or involve some aspect of a 'feeling-state' as part of the content of the insight itself. This would be consistent with the point of view discussed earlier in this chapter when we remarked that 'it would appear that therapeutic change as a consequence of analysis depends, to a large degree, on the provision of a structured and organized conceptual and affective framework within which the patient can effectively place himself and his subjective experience of himself and others'. This would permit us to understand how

119

different psychoanalytic and psychotherapeutic points of view, as mirrored in the interpretations given to the patient, may at times prove equally effective from the point of view of therapeutic results.

Chapter 11

Working Through

Psychoanalytic treatment shares with some other forms of psychotherapy the aim of bringing about lasting changes within the
patient. In common with other 'insight' therapies it makes use of
interpretations and other verbal interventions (Chap. 10). While
these are aimed partly at making unconscious content and processes conscious, it has been maintained since the early days of
psychoanalytic treatment that 'making what is unconscious
conscious' and the gaining of insight are not sufficient, in the
ordinary course of events, to bring about a fundamental change in
the patient. In contrast to procedures involving hypnosis and
massive abreaction (catharsis), the psychoanalytic method is
regarded as depending for its success on a number of additional
elements. Some of these have been discussed in previous chapters,
particularly the elements of treatment alliance (Chap. 3), transference (Chaps. 4 and 5), and the analysis of resistance (Chap. 7).
It is the purpose of the present chapter to examine those further
factors in the psychoanalytic treatment situation which have been
encompassed under the heading of *working through*.

Although Freud had used such terms as 'wearing away' and
'working over' in his earliest psychoanalytic writings (1895), the
clinical concept of working through was introduced in a paper on
'Remembering, repeating and working-through' (1914a). There
Freud pointed out that the aim of treatment during the first phase
of psychoanalysis had been the recall of the pathogenic traumatic
event thought to lie behind the neurosis, and the abreaction of the
dammed-up affect associated with that event. With the giving-up
of hypnosis, the therapeutic task became that of recovering signi-

ficant forgotten mental content and associated affects through the patient's free associations, and this called for an 'expenditure of work' on the part of the patient because of his resistances to uncovering what was repressed. The recall of significant memories gave way, in prime importance, to the *repetition* of these in the form of transference and acting out (Chap. 9). The analytic work was now regarded as being in large part directed towards the interpretation of the patient's resistances as well as being concerned with showing the patient how the past repeats itself in the present. However, even if the analyst has uncovered a resistance and shown it to the patient, this in itself will not cause the treatment to progress.

'One must allow the patient time to become more conversant with this resistance with which he has now become acquainted, to *work through* it, to overcome it, by continuing, in defiance of it, the analytic work according to the fundamental rule of analysis. . . . This working-through of the resistances may in practice turn out to be an arduous task for the subject of the analysis and a trial of patience for the analyst. Nevertheless it is a part of the work which effects the greatest changes in the patient and which distinguishes analytic treatment from any kind of treatment by suggestion' (Freud, 1914a).

Although Freud later differentiated a number of different sources of resistance (Chap. 7), he came to link the need for working through with the particular form of resistance which follows from the 'compulsion to repeat' (1920), and the so-called 'id-resistance' (1926a). This can be regarded as a reflection of the 'opposition' of the instinctual impulses to detachment from their previous objects and modes of discharge (1915a, c). Freud also wrote (borrowing a term from Jung) of 'psychical inertia' (1918), of 'adhesiveness' (1916–17) and 'sluggishness' (1940) of the libido as forces operating against recovery.* In 1937 he related 'psychical inertia' to inherent constitutional factors and to ageing (1937a). Ageing was thought to make the psychoanalytic process less effective, so that old age is regarded as a contra-indication for psychoanalytic treatment (Tyson and Sandler, 1971).

* These terms reflect Freud's concept of instinctual impulses as energy which can be attached to particular mental representations, in particular those of the childhood love-objects. This conceptualization has come under attack in recent years (e.g. Rosenblatt and Thickstun, 1970).

Thus, for Freud, 'working through' represented the work entailed (for both analyst and patient) in overcoming resistances to change due primarily to the tendency for the instinctual drives to cling to accustomed patterns of discharge. Working through represented analytic work which was *additional* to that involved in uncovering conflicts and resistances. Intellectual insight without working through was not regarded as sufficient for the therapeutic task, as the tendency for the previous modes of functioning to repeat themselves in accustomed ways would remain.

Developments in psychoanalytic theory after Freud have affected the concept in various ways, so that some of its original descriptive simplicity has been lost. Indeed, Novey has written (1962) of 'our failure to understand the process of working through', and more recently Bird (*in* Schmale, 1966) has expressed the view that there is no need for such a term. However, the term continues to be widely used and is fairly generally regarded as a basic psychoanalytic clinical or technical concept.

Fenichel (1937, 1941) regarded working through as an activity of the analyst rather than of both analyst and patient, and referred to it as 'a special type of interpretation'. He pointed out that the patient will show repeated resistance to the awareness of unconscious material which had previously been interpreted, and the work of interpretation has itself to be repeated, even though the process may now go more quickly and easily than before. While at times exactly the same picture may reappear in the patient, at other times *variants* may occur in different contexts. 'The process that requires demonstrating to patients the same thing again and again at different times or in various connections, is called, following Freud, "working-through" ' (1941).

It is of interest that although Fenichel narrows Freud's concept in restricting working through to a type of interpretation, he widens it by relating it as well to the resistance of the ego and superego to change. Further, in agreement with a number of other authors, he goes on to liken working through to the process of *mourning*.

'A person who has lost a friend must in all situations which remind him of this lost friend make clear to himself anew that he has this friend no longer and that a renunciation is necessary. The conception of this friend *has representation* in many complexes of memories and wishes, and the detachment from the friend must take place separately in each complex' (1941).

Fenichel, following Freud (1914a), saw working through as resulting in the freeing of small quantities of the 'energy' attached to the representation, being in this way similar to abreaction, although quite the opposite of the single massive abreaction. At the same time, he spoke of interpretation as having the effect of 'educating the patient to produce steadily less distorted derivatives . . . ' (1937). Since Fenichel, what one might call the 'micro-abreaction' aspect of working through has received relatively little consideration. In contrast, the 'learning' aspect has moved more into the foreground.

Further authors have emphasized the (at times laborious) tracing of the ramifications of a conflict in different areas of the patient's life as fundamental to working through. As Fromm-Reichmann put it: ' . . . any understanding, any new piece of awareness which has been gained by interpretive clarification, has to be reconquered and tested time and again in new connections and contacts with other interlocking experiences, which may or may not have to be approached interpretively in their own right' (1950).

In 1956 Greenacre stressed the importance of working through in those cases where a childhood traumatic event has had extensive effects in different areas of the personality. She pointed out that

'It was early recognized that if the infantile memories were recovered too quickly, or were *acted out* in the transference and not adequately interpreted, the abreaction at the time might be appreciable, but had no lasting effect. In such instances, the working through had not seemed necessary for the recovery of the memory, but now became essential to sustain any therapeutic effect – not to diminish the resistance and *reach* the memory, but to demonstrate again and again to the patient the working of instinctual trends in various situations in life.'

Greenacre comments that 'the defensive conflict remained somewhat structured unless worked with repetitively and in connection with its effect in various situations. . . .' She also suggests that increased emphasis on the analysis of the mechanisms of defence has led to 'the recognition of the need for consistent work with the patterns of defence. . . . This has taken over much of what would previously have been referred to as *working through*.'

In the same year Kris (1956) pointed out that the work of interpretation leads eventually to reconstruction of the patient's past, and an aspect of working through is the need to apply these reconstructions to many different areas and levels of the patient's material. Related to this is the more general point made by Loewald (1960), who sees analysis as a process leading to structural changes in the patient.* But

'the analyst structures and articulates . . . the material and the productions offered by the patient. If an interpretation of unconscious meaning is timely, the words by which this meaning is expressed are recognizable to the patient as expressions of what he experiences. They organize for him what was previously less organized and thus give him the "distance" from himself which enables him to understand, to see, to put into words and to "handle" what was previously not visible, understandable, speakable, tangible. . . . The analyst functions as a representative of a higher stage of organization and mediates this to the patient, insofar as the analyst's understanding is attuned to what is, and the way in which it is, in need of organization.'†

In a cogent discussion of working through, Novey (1962) considers the difficulties surrounding the concept, and suggests that there are factors involved between analyst and patient which psychoanalysis has in common with other therapies, and which make for working through. These factors (supportive techniques, etc.) operate and appear to be necessary over and above the giving of correct interpretations. Novey comments that working through occurs outside the analytic session. 'Much of what we would consider working through in its proper sense is the time involved in actually experiencing and re-experiencing in intellectual as well as affective terms, so as to bring about constructive change.' A

* The term 'structure' is used in the psychoanalytic literature to refer specifically to the trio of id, ego and superego, but is nowadays used more generally to denote 'psychological organizations with a slow rate of change'.

† Loewald's formulation of this aspect of the analyst's function allows us to consider the theoretical framework and techniques of the analyst not from the point of view of whether it is 'right' or 'wrong', but whether they are *useful* in the sense described.

similar point is made by Valenstein in regard to the 'work' which may go on after an analysis has ended. 'As working-through goes on apace during that unending phase of self-analytic work which follows the conclusion of the analysis in its formal form, these new action patterns, as well as new thought and affect patterns, develop an increasing degree of structuralization (1962).'

Both Stewart (1963) and Greenson (1965b) adhere to Freud's view that working through is primarily directed against 'id-resistance'. However, Greenson arrives at a definition of working through centred around insight and change.

'We do not regard the analytic work as working through before the patient has insight, only after. It is the goal of working through to make insight effective, i.e. to make significant and lasting changes in the patient. . . . The analysis of those resistances which keep insight from leading to change is the work of working through. The analyst and the patient each contributes to this work . . . working through is essentially the repetition, deepening, and extension of the analysis of the resistances.'

The blurring of the concept of working through appears to have come about as a consequence of the failure of many psychoanalytic writers to maintain a clear differentiation between working through as a *description* of an important part of the psychoanalytic therapeutic work, and the *psychological processes* which bring about the need for, and which follow on working through. The 'arduous task' for the subject and the 'trial of patience' for the analyst (Freud, 1914a) in covering the same ground over and over again, in tracing the ramifications of unconscious impulses, conflicts, fantasies and defences as these appear and reappear in the patient's material, seems to be the essence of working through. Such a description of working through would probably be acceptable to most psychoanalysts, but disagreement appears to arise as soon as the concept is broadened. These disagreements reflect different theoretical orientations within psychoanalysis, and the emphasis on different aspects of mental functioning at various times in the history of psychoanalytic theory. Freud was careful to distinguish between working through, the factors which were thought to make it necessary (in particular, the 'id-resistance') and the results which it was considered to bring about (changes more permanent than those obtained by sugges-

126

tion or abreaction only). However, such authors as Greenacre (1956) apparently contrast the repetitive aspects of the analysis of defensive patterns with working through. Similarly, Greenson (1965b) sees working through as the *result* of 'so many procedures performed simultaneously by the analyst and the patient . . .' but at the same time restricts it to the analysis of those resistances which keep insight from leading to change.

It would appear to be useful to retain working through as an essentially descriptive clinical concept. It has been regarded as a necessary part of the psychoanalytic therapeutic process, and is related to the need to overcome resistances from all sources. However, the failure of the patient to change following interpretation or insight may be due to factors other than resistance.* The need for reinforcement and reward in order to accomplish learning (including learning through 'insight') and to bring about the formation of new structures, and the inhibition or extinction of old ones (Sandler and Joffe, 1968) is relevant in this connection. Such learning and modification of structures would not be part of working through, but a consequence of it.

It is perhaps worth commenting that psychoanalytic writers uniformly maintain that although working through is an essential part of the psychoanalytic process, interpretation of unconscious mental content and of transference repetitions, together with the gaining of insight, are equally vital to it. Thus any technique which does not make use of all of these elements would not be regarded as psychoanalytic. However, this is not to say that working through cannot play a role in other forms of therapy, in particular those which involve an element of 'retraining' or 're-education'.

---

* The concept of resistance is another instance of a descriptive concept which has been given explanatory power. We have previously emphasized the need to distinguish between *forms* of resistance and *sources* of resistance, and in regard to the latter have suggested that so-called 'id-resistance' is a special instance of the more general resistance to the giving up of past adaptive solutions (including neurotic symptoms) due to the need for 'unlearning' or extinction (Chap. 7).

References

ABRAHAM, K. (1908). 'The Psycho-sexual Differences between Hysteria and Dementia Praecox, *Selected Papers on Psycho-Analysis*, London: Hogarth Press, 1927.

ABRAHAM, K. (1919). 'A Particular Form of Neurotic Resistance Against the Psycho-Analytic Method, *Selected Papers on Psycho-Analysis*, London: Hogarth Press, 1927.

ABT, L. and WEISSMAN, S. (ed.) (1965). *Acting Out : Theoretical and Clinical Aspects*, New York: Grune & Stratton Inc.

ALEXANDER, F. (1925). 'A Metapsychological Description of the Process of Cure', *International Journal of Psycho-Analysis*, 6, 13–34.

ALEXANDER, F. (1948). *Fundamentals of Psychoanalysis*, New York: W. W. Norton & Co. Inc.

ALEXANDER, F. (1950). 'Analysis of the Therapeutic Factors in Psychoanalytic Treatment', *Psychoanalytic Quarterly*, 19, 482–500.

ALEXANDER, F. and FRENCH, T. M. (1946). *Psychoanalytic Therapy*, New York: Ronald Press Co.

ARKIN, F. S. (1960). Discussion of Salzman, L. 'The Negative Therapeutic Reaction', in Masserman, J. H. (ed.), *Science and Psychoanalysis*, 3, 314–17.

ARLOW, J. A. and BRENNER, C. (1964). *Psychoanalytic Concepts and the Structural Theory*, New York: International Universities Press Inc.

ARLOW, J. A. and BRENNER, C. (1969). 'The Psychopathology of the Psychoses: a Proposed Revision', *International Journal of Psycho-Analysis*, 50, 5–14.

ATKINS, N. B. (1967). 'Comments on Severe and Psychotic Regression in Analysis', *Journal of the American Psychoanalytic Association*, 15, 584–605.

BALINT, M. (1933). 'On Transference of Emotions', *Primary Love and Psycho-Analytic Technique*, London: Tavistock Publications Ltd, 1965.

BALINT, M. (1934). 'Charakteranalyse und Neubeginn', *Internationale Zeitschrift für Psychoanalyse*, 20, 54–65.

BALINT, M. (1949). 'Changing Therapeutical Aims and Techniques in Psycho-Analysis', *Primary Love and Psycho-Analytic Technique*, London: Tavistock Publications Ltd, 1965.

BALINT, M. (1965). 'The Benign and Malignant Forms of Regression', *New Perspectives in Psychoanalysis*, George E. Daniel (ed.), New York: Grune & Stratton Inc.

BALINT, M. (1968). *The Basic Fault, Therapeutic Aspects of Regression*, London: Tavistock Publications Ltd.

BALINT, M. and BALINT, A. (1939). 'On Transference and Counter-Transference', *Primary Love and Psycho-Analytic Technique*, London: Tavistock Publications Ltd, 1965.

BATESON, G., JACKSON, D. D., HALEY, J. and WEAKLAND, J. (1956). 'Towards a Theory of Schizophrenia', *Behavioral Science*, 1, 251–64.

BELLAK, L. (1965). 'The Concept of Acting Out: Theoretical Considerations', *Acting Out: Theoretical and Clinical Aspects*, Abt, L. and Weissman, S. (ed.), New York: Grune & Stratton Inc.

BIBRING, E. (1954). 'Psychoanalysis and the Dynamic Psychotherapies', *Journal of the American Psychoanalytic Association*, 2, 745–70.

BION, W. R. (1961). *Experiences in Groups*, London: Tavistock Publications Ltd, 1968.

BION, W. R. (1962). *Learning from Experience*, London: Wm. Heinemann Ltd.

BLEULER, E. (1911). *Dementia Praecox oder Gruppe der Schizophrenien*, Leipzig. (Transl. *Dementia Praecox or the Group of Schizophrenias*, New York: International Universities Press, 1950).

BLOS, P. (1966). Discussion remarks in *A Developmental Approach to Problems of Acting Out*, E. Rexford (ed.). Monographs of the American Academy of Child Psychiatry, No. 1.

BRENNER, C. (1959). 'The Masochistic Character: Genesis and Treatment', *Journal of the American Psychoanalytic Association*, 7, 197–226.

BROWN, G. W., BONE, M., DALISON, B. and WING, J. K. (1966). *Schizophrenia and Social Care: A Comparative Follow-up Study of 339 Schizophrenic Patients*, London: Oxford University Press.

CESIO, F. R. (1956). 'Un caso de reacción terapeutica negativa', *Revista de psicoanálisis*, 13, 522–6.

CESIO, F. R. (1958). 'La reacción terapeutica negativa', *Revista de psicoanálisis*, 15, 293–9.

CESIO, F. R. (1960a). 'El letargo, un contribución al estudio de la reacción terapeutica negativa', *Revista de psicoanálisis*, 17, 10–26.

CESIO, F. R. (1960b). 'Contribución al estudio de la reacción terapeutica negativa', *Revista de psicoanálisis*, 17, 289–98.

COHEN, M. B. (1952). 'Counter-transference and Anxiety', *Psychiatry*, 15, 231–43.

DEUTSCH, H. (1939). 'A Discussion of Certain Forms of Resistance', *International Journal of Psycho-Analysis*, 20, 72–83.

DEUTSCH, H. (1966). Discussion remarks in *A Developmental Approach to*

Problems of Acting Out, E. Rexford (ed.). Monographs of the American Academy of Child Psychiatry, No. 1.

DICKES, R. (1967). 'Severe Regressive Disruptions of the Therapeutic Alliance, *Journal of the American Psychoanalytic Association*, 15, 508–33.

EIDELBERG, L. (1948). 'A Contribution to the Study of Masochism', *Studies in Psychoanalysis*, New York: International Universities Press Inc.

EIDELBERG, L. (ed.) (1968). *Encyclopedia of Psychoanalysis*, New York: The Free Press.

EISSLER, K. R. (1953). 'The Effect of the Structure of the Ego on Psychoanalytic Technique', *Journal of the American Psychoanalytic Association*, 1, 104–43.

ENGLISH, O. S. and PEARSON, G. H. (1937). *Common Neuroses of Children and Adults*, New York: W. W. Norton & Co. Inc.

ERIKSON, E. (1950). *Child and Society*, New York: W. W. Norton & Co. Inc.

FEDERN, P. (1943). 'Psychoanalysis of Psychoses', *Psychiatric Quarterly*, 17, 3–19, 246–57 and 470–87.

FEIGENBAUM, D. (1934). 'Clinical Fragments', *Psychoanalytic Quarterly*, 3, 363–90.

FENICHEL, O. (1937). 'Symposium on the Therapeutic Results of Psychoanalysis', *Collected Papers*, Vol. 2, 19–24, London: Routledge & Kegan Paul, 1954.

FENICHEL, O. (1941). *Problems of Psychoanalytic Technique*, New York: The Psychoanalytic Quarterly Inc.

FENICHEL, O. (1945a). *The Psychoanalytic Theory of Neurosis*, London: Routledge & Kegan Paul.

FENICHEL, O. (1945b). 'Neurotic Acting Out', *Psychoanalytic Review*, 32, 197–206.

FERENCZI, S. (1912). 'Transitory Symptom-constructions During the Analysis' (transitory conversion, substitution, illusion, hallucination, 'character-regression', and 'expression-displacement'), *Sex in Psychoanalysis*, New York: Basic Books, 1950.

FERENCZI, S. (1914). 'Falling Asleep During the Analysis', *Further Contributions to the Theory and Technique of Psychoanalysis*, London: Hogarth Press, 1926.

FLIESS, R. (1953). 'Counter-transference and Counter-identification', *Journal of the American Psychoanalytic Association*, 1, 268–84.

FRENCH, T. M. (1939). 'Insight and Distortion in Dreams', *International Journal of Psycho-Analysis*, 20, 287–98.

FREUD, ANNA (1928). *Introduction to the Technique of Child Analysis*, New York and Washington: Nervous and Mental Disease Publishing Co.

131

FREUD, ANNA (1936). *The Ego and the Mechanisms of Defence*, London: Hogarth Press.

FREUD, ANNA (1965). *Normality and Pathology in Childhood*. London: Hogarth Press, 1966.

FREUD, ANNA (1968). 'Acting Out', *International Journal of Psycho-Analysis*, *49*, 165–70.

FREUD, S. (1887–1902). *The Origins of Psycho-Analysis*, Standard Edition, *1*, London: Hogarth Press.

FREUD, S. (1895). *Studies on Hysteria*, Standard Edition, *2*, London: Hogarth Press.

FREUD, S. (1896). 'Further Remarks on the Neuro-psychoses of Defence', Standard Edition, *3*, London: Hogarth Press.

FREUD, S. (1900). *The Interpretation of Dreams*, Standard Edition, *4–5*, London: Hogarth Press.

FREUD, S. (1901). *The Psychopathology of Everyday Life*, Standard Edition, *6*, London: Hogarth Press.

FREUD, S. (1904). 'Freud's Psycho-Analytic Procedure', Standard Edition, *7*, London: Hogarth Press.

FREUD, S. (1905a). *Three Essays on the Theory of Sexuality*, Standard Edition, *7*, London: Hogarth Press.

FREUD, S. (1905b). 'Fragment of an Analysis of a Case of Hysteria', Standard Edition, *7*, London: Hogarth Press.

FREUD, S. (1909a). *Five Lectures on Psycho-Analysis*, Standard Edition, *11*, London: Hogarth Press.

FREUD, S. (1909b). 'Analysis of a Phobia in a Five-year-old Boy', Standard Edition, *10*, London: Hogarth Press.

FREUD, S. (1909c). 'Notes Upon a Case of Obsessional Neurosis', Standard Edition, *10*, London: Hogarth Press.

FREUD, S. (1910a). 'The Future Prospects of Psycho-Analytic Therapy' Standard Edition, *11*, London: Hogarth Press.

FREUD, S. (1910b). Letter to Ferenczi of 6 Oct. 1910, quoted in Jones, E. *Sigmund Freud: Life and Work*, Vol. 2, New York: Basic Books, 1955.

FREUD, S. (1911a). 'Psycho-analytic notes on an autobiographical account of a case of paranoia (dementia paranoides)', Standard Edition, *12*, London: Hogarth Press.

FREUD, S. (1911b). 'The Handling of Dream-interpretation in Psycho-Analysis', Standard Edition, *12*, London: Hogarth Press.

FREUD, S. (1912a). 'The Dynamics of Transference', Standard Edition, *12*, London: Hogarth Press.

FREUD, S. (1912b). 'Recommendations to Physicians Practising Psycho-Analysis', Standard Edition, *12*, London: Hogarth Press.

FREUD, S. (1913a). 'On Beginning the Treatment', Standard Edition, *12*, London: Hogarth Press.

FREUD, S. (1913b). 'The Disposition to Obsessional Neurosis', Standard Edition, *12*, London: Hogarth Press.

FREUD, S. (1914a). 'Remembering, Repeating and Working-Through', Standard Edition, *12*, London: Hogarth Press.

FREUD, S. (1914b). 'On Narcissism: an Introduction', Standard Edition, *14*, London: Hogarth Press.

FREUD, S. (1915a). 'Observations on Transference-love', Standard Edition, *12*, London: Hogarth Press.

FREUD, S. (1915b). 'Instincts and Their Vicissitudes', Standard Edition, *14*, London: Hogarth Press.

FREUD, S. (1915c). 'A Case of Paranoia Running Counter to the Psycho-Analytic Theory of the Disease', Standard Edition, *14*, London: Hogarth Press.

FREUD, S. (1916). 'Some Character-types Met With in Psycho-Analytic Work', Standard Edition, *14*, London: Hogarth Press.

FREUD, S. (1916–17). *Introductory Lectures on Psycho-Analysis*, Standard Edition, 15–16, London: Hogarth Press.

FREUD, S. (1918). 'From the History of an Infantile Neurosis', Standard Edition, *17*, London: Hogarth Press.

FREUD, S. (1920). *Beyond the Pleasure Principle*, Standard Edition, *18* London: Hogarth Press.

FREUD, S. (1921). *Group Psychology and the Analysis of the Ego*, Standard Edition, *18*, London: Hogarth Press.

FREUD, S. (1923). *The Ego and the Id*, Standard Edition, *19*, London: Hogarth Press.

FREUD, S. (1924). 'The Economic Problem of Masochism', Standard Edition, *19*, London: Hogarth Press.

FREUD, S. (1925). *An Autobiographical Study*, Standard Edition, *20*, London: Hogarth Press.

FREUD, S. (1926a). *Inhibitions, Symptoms and Anxiety*, Standard Edition, *20*, London: Hogarth Press.

FREUD, S. (1926b). *The Question of Lay Analysis*, Standard Edition, *20*, London: Hogarth Press.

FREUD, S. (1931). 'Female Sexuality', Standard Edition, *21*, London: Hogarth Press.

FREUD, S. (1933). *New Introductory Lectures on Psycho-Analysis*, Standard Edition, *22*, London: Hogarth Press.

FREUD, S. (1937a). 'Analysis Terminable and Interminable', Standard Edition, *23*, London: Hogarth Press.

FREUD, S. (1937b). 'Constructions in Analysis', Standard Edition, *23*, London: Hogarth Press.

FREUD, S. (1939). *Moses and Monotheism*, Standard Edition, *23*, London: Hogarth Press.

THE PATIENT AND THE ANALYST

FREUD, S. (1940). *An Outline of Psycho-Analysis*, Standard Edition *23*, London: Hogarth Press.

FRIEDMAN, L. (1969). 'The Therapeutic Alliance', *International Journal of Psycho-Analysis, 50*, 139–53.

FROMM-REICHMANN, F. (1950). *Principles of Intensive Psychotherapy*, Chicago: University Press.

FROSCH, J. (1967). 'Severe Regressive States During Analysis', *Journal of the American Psychoanalytic Association, 15*, 491–507 and 606–25.

GERÖ, G. (1936). 'The Construction of Depression', *International Journal of Psycho-Analysis, 17*, 423–61.

GERÖ, G. (1951). 'The Concept of Defence', *Psychoanalytic Quarterly, 20*, 565–78.

GILL, M. (1954). 'Psychoanalysis and Exploratory Psychotherapy', *Journal of the American Psychoanalytic Association, 2*, 771–97.

GITELSON, M. (1952). 'The Emotional Position of the Analyst in the Psycho-Analytic Situation', *International Journal of Psycho-Analysis, 33*, 1–10.

GITELSON, M. (1954). 'Therapeutic Problems in the Analysis of the "Normal" Candidate', *International Journal of Psycho-Analysis, 35*, 174–83.

GITELSON, M. (1962). 'The Curative Factors in Psychoanalysis', *International Journal of Psycho-Analysis, 43*, 194–205.

GLOVER, E. (1931). 'The Therapeutic Effect of Inexact Interpretation', *International Journal of Psycho-Analysis, 12*, 397–411.

GLOVER, E. (1937). 'The Theory of the Therapeutic Results of Psychoanalysis', *International Journal of Psycho-Analysis, 18*, 125–32.

GLOVER, E. (1945). 'Examination of the Klein System of Child Psychology' *Psychoanalytic Study of the Child, 1*, 75–118.

GLOVER, E. (1955). *The Technique of Psycho-Analysis*, London: Baillière, Tindall & Cox.

GREENACRE, P. (1950). 'General Problems of Acting Out', *Psychoanalytic Quarterly, 19*, 455–67.

GREENACRE, P. (1956). 'Re-evaluation of the Process of Working Through', *International Journal of Psycho-Analysis, 37*, 439–44.

GREENBAUM, H. (1956). 'Combined Psychoanalytic Therapy with Negative Therapeutic Reactions', Rifkin, A. H. (ed.), *Schizophrenia in Psychoanalytic Office Practice*, 56–65, New York: Grune & Stratton.

GREENSON, R. R. (1965a). 'The Working Alliance and the Transference Neurosis', *Psychoanalytic Quarterly, 34*, 155–81.

GREENSON, R. R. (1965b). 'The Problem of Working Through', Schur M. (ed.), *Drives, Affects, Behavior*, New York: International Universities Press.

134

GREENSON, R. R. (1967). *The Technique and Practice of Psychoanalysis*, Vol. 1, New York: International Universities Press.

GREENSON, R. R. and WEXLER, M. (1969). 'The Non-transference Relationship in the Psychoanalytic Situation', *International Journal of Psycho-Analysis*, *50*, 27–39.

HAMMETT, VAN BUREN O. (1961). 'Delusional Transference', *American Journal of Psychotherapy*, *15*, 574–81.

HARTMANN, H. (1939). *Ego Psychology and the Problem of Adaptation*, London: Imago, 1958.

HARTMANN, H. (1944). 'Psychoanalysis and Sociology', *Essays on Ego Psychology*, London: Hogarth Press, 1964.

HARTMANN, H. (1951). 'Technical implications of ego psychology', *Psychoanalytic Quarterly*, *20*, 31–43.

HARTMANN, H. (1956). 'The Development of the Ego Concept in Freud's Work', *International Journal of Psycho-Analysis*, *37*, 425–38.

HARTMANN, H. (1964). *Essays on Ego Psychology*, London: Hogarth Press.

HEIMANN, P. (1950). 'On Counter-transference', *International Journal of Psycho-Analysis*, *31*, 81–4.

HEIMANN, P. (1960). 'Counter-transference', *British Journal of Medical Psychology*, *33*, 9–15.

HILL, D. (1956). 'Psychiatry', Richardson, J. S. (ed.), *The Practice of Medicine*, London: J. & A. Churchill Ltd.

HILL, D. (1968). 'Depression: Disease, Reaction or Posture?' *American Journal of Psychiatry*, *125*, 445–57.

HILL, D. (1969). 'Psychiatric Education During a Period of Social Change', *British Medical Journal*, *1*, 205–209.

HINSIE, L. E. and CAMPBELL, R. J. (1970). *Psychiatric Dictionary*, (4th edition), London: Oxford University Press.

HOFFER, W. (1956). 'Transference and Transference Neurosis', *International Journal of Psycho-Analysis*, *37*, 377–9.

HOLDER, A. (1970). 'Conceptual Problems of Acting Out in Children', *Journal of Child Psychotherapy*, *2*, 5–22.

HORNEY, K. (1936). 'The Problem of the Negative Therapeutic Reaction', *Psychoanalytic Quarterly*, *5*, 29–44.

ISAACS, S. (1939). 'Criteria for Interpretation', *International Journal of Psycho-Analysis*, *20*, 148–60.

IVIMEY, M. (1948). 'Negative Therapeutic Reaction', *American Journal of Psychoanalysis*, *8*, 24–33.

JASPERS, K. (1913). *Allgemeine Psychopathologie*, Berlin: Springer Verlag.

JOFFE, W. G. (1969). 'A Critical Review of the Status of the Envy Concept', *International Journal of Psycho-Analysis*, *50*, 533–45.

135

JOFFE, W. G. and SANDLER, J. (1965). 'Notes on Pain, Depression and Individuation', *Psychoanalytic Study of the Child*, 20, 394–424.

JOFFE, W. G. and SANDLER, J. (1967). 'On the Concept of Pain, with Special Reference to Depression and Psychogenic Pain', *Journal of Psychosomatic Research*, 11, 69–75.

JONES, E. (1953). *The Life and Work of Sigmund Freud*, Vol. 1, London: Hogarth Press.

JUNG, C. G. (1907). *Ueber die Psychologie der Dementia Praecox: Ein Versuch*, Halle a.S. (transl. *The Psychology of Dementia Praecox*, in *Collected Works*, 3, London, 1960).

KAPLAN, A. (1964). *The Conduct of Inquiry*, San Francisco: Chandler Publishing Co.

KEMPER, W. W. (1966). 'Transference and Counter-transference as a Functional Unit', *Official Report on Pan-American Congress for Psychoanalysis*, August 1966.

KEPECS, J. G. (1966). 'Theories of Transference Neurosis', *Psychoanalytic Quarterly*, 35, 497–521.

KERNBERG, O. (1965). 'Notes on Countertransference', *Journal of the American Psychoanalytic Association*, 13, 38–56.

KHAN, M. (1960). 'Regression and Integration in the Analytic Setting', *International Journal of Psycho-Analysis*, 41, 130–46.

KHAN, M. (1963). 'Silence as Communication', *Bulletin of the Menninger Clinic*, 27, 300–17.

KLEIN, M. (1932). *The Psycho-Analysis of Children*, London: Hogarth Press.

KLEIN, M. (1948). *Contributions to Psychoanalysis*, London: Hogarth Press.

KÖHLER, W. (1925). *The Mentality of Apes*, New York: Harcourt, Brace & World Inc.

KRAEPELIN, E. (1906). *Lectures on Clinical Psychiatry*, New York: Hafner, 1969.

KRIS, E. (1951). 'Ego Psychology and Interpretation in Psychoanalytic Therapy', *Psychoanalytic Quarterly*, 20, 15–29.

KRIS, E. (1952). *Explorations in Art*, New York: International Universities Press.

KRIS, E. (1956). 'The Recovery of Childhood Memories in Psychoanalysis', *Psychoanalytic Study of the Child*, 11, 54–88.

KUBIE, L. S. (1950). *Practical and Theoretical Aspects of Psychoanalysis*, New York: International Universities Press.

LAPLANCHE, J. and PONTALIS, J. B. (1967). *Vocabulaire de la Psychanalyse*, Paris: Presses Universitaires de France.

LEWIN, B. (1950). *The Psychoanalysis of Elation*, New York: W. W. Norton & Co. Inc.

LEWIN, B. (1961). 'Reflections on Depression', *Psychoanalytic Study of the Child*, *16*, 321–31.

LIDZ, T., FLECK, S. and CORNELISON, A. (ed.) (1965). *Schizophrenia and the Family*, New York: International Universities Press.

LIMENTANI, A. (1966). 'A Re-evaluation of Acting Out in Relation to Working Through', *International Journal of Psycho-Analysis*, *47*, 274–82.

LITTLE, M. (1951). 'Counter transference and the Patient's Response to it', *International Journal of Psycho-Analysis*, *32*, 32–40.

LITTLE, M. (1958). 'On Delusional Transference (transference psychosis)', *International Journal of Psycho-Analysis*, *39*, 134–8.

LITTLE, M. (1960a). 'On Basic Unity', *International Journal of Psycho-Analysis*, *41*, 377–84.

LITTLE, M. (1960b). 'Countertransference', *British Journal of Medical Psychology*, *33*, 29–31.

LITTLE, M. (1966). 'Transference in Borderline States', *International Journal of Psycho-Analysis*, *47*, 476–85.

LOEWALD, H. W. (1960). 'On the Therapeutic Action of Psychoanalysis', *International Journal of Psycho-Analysis*, *41*, 16–33.

LOEWENSTEIN, R. M. (1951). 'The Problem of Interpretation', *Psychoanalytic Quarterly*, *20*, 1–14.

LOEWENSTEIN, R. M. (1954). 'Some Remarks on Defences, Autonomous Ego and Psycho-Analytic Technique', *International Journal of Psycho-Analysis*, *35*, 188–93.

LOEWENSTEIN, R. M. (1969). 'Developments in the Theory of Transference in the Last Fifty Years', *International Journal of Psycho-Analysis*, *50*, 583–8

LORAND, S. (1958). 'Resistance', *Psychoanalytic Quarterly*, *27*, 462–4.

MAIN, T. F. (1957). 'The Ailment', *British Journal of Medical Psychology*, *30*, 129–45.

MARTIN, A. R. (1952). 'The Dynamics of Insight', *American Journal of Psychoanalysis*, *12*, 24–38.

MELTZER, D. (1967). *The Psycho-Analytical Process*. London: Wm. Heinemann Ltd.

MENNINGER, K. (1958). *Theory of Psychoanalytic Technique*. New York: Basic Books.

MISHLER, E. G. and WAXLER, N. E. (1966). 'Family Interaction Patterns and Schizophrenia: a Review of Current Theories', *International Journal of Psychiatry*, *2*, 375–413.

MONEY-KYRLE, R. E. (1956). 'Normal Counter-transference and Some of its Deviations', *International Journal of Psycho-Analysis*, *37*, 360–6.

MOORE, B. E. and FINE, B.D. (1967). *A Glossary of Psychoanalytic Terms and Concepts*, New York: American Psychoanalytic Association.

MYERSON, P. A. (1960). 'Awareness and Stress: Post-psycho-analytic Utilization of Insight', *International Journal of Psycho-Analysis, 41,* 147–56.

MYERSON, P. A. (1963). 'Assimilation of Unconscious Material', *International Journal of Psycho-Analysis, 44,* 317–27.

MYERSON, P. A. (1965). 'Modes of Insight', *Journal of the American Psychoanalytic Association, 13,* 771–92.

NOVEY, S. (1962). 'The Principle of "Working Through" in Psychoanalysis', *Journal of the American Psychoanalytic Association, 10,* 658–76.

NOVEY, S. (1968). *The Second Look,* Baltimore: Johns Hopkins Press.

NUNBERG, H. (1920). 'The Course of the Libidinal Conflict in a Case of Schizophrenia', *Practice and Theory of Psychoanalysis,* New York: International Universities Press, 1948.

NUNBERG, H. (1951). 'Transference and Reality', *International Journal of Psycho-Analysis, 32,* 1–9.

OLINICK, S. L. (1954). 'Some Considerations of the Use of Questioning as a Psychoanalytic Technique', *Journal of the American Psychoanalytic Association, 2,* 57–66.

OLINICK, S. L. (1964). 'The Negative Therapeutic Reaction', *International Journal of Psycho-Analysis, 45,* 540–8.

ORR, D. W. (1954). 'Transference and Countertransference: a Historical Survey', *Journal of the American Psychoanalytic Association, 2,* 621–70.

PRESSMAN, M. (1969a). 'The Cognitive Function of the Ego in Psychoanalysis: I. The Search for Insight', *International Journal of Psycho-Analysis, 50,* 187–96.

PRESSMAN, M. (1969b). 'The Cognitive Function of the Ego in Psychoanalysis: II. Repression, Incognizance and Insight Formation', *International Journal of Psycho-Analysis, 50,* 343–51.

RANGELL, L. (1968). 'A Point of View on Acting Out', *International Journal of Psycho-Analysis, 49,* 195–201.

RAPAPORT, D. (1959). 'A Historical Survey of Ego Psychology', *Identity and the Life Cycle,* Erikson E., New York: International Universities Press.

RAPPAPORT, E. A. (1956). 'The Management of an Erotized Transference', *Psychoanalytic Quarterly, 25,* 515–29.

REICH, A. (1951). 'On Counter-transference', *International Journal of Psycho-Analysis, 32,* 25–31.

REICH, A. (1960). 'Further Remarks on Countertransference', *International Journal of Psycho-Analysis, 41,* 389–95.

REICH, W. (1928). 'On Character Analysis', *The Psycho-Analytic Reader,* R. Fliess (ed.), London: Hogarth Press, 1950.

REICH, W. (1929). 'The Genital Character and the Neurotic Character', *The Psycho-Analytic Reader*, R. Fliess (ed.), London: Hogarth Press, 1950.

REICH, W. (1933). *Charakteranalyse*, Vienna: Selbstverlag.

REICH, W. (1934). *Psychischer Kontakt und vegetative Strömung*, Copenhagen: Sexpol Verlag.

REID, J. R. and FINESINGER, J. E. (1952). 'The Role of Insight in Psychotherapy', *American Journal of Psychiatry*, *108*, 726–34.

REIDER, N. (1957). 'Transference Psychosis', *Journal of the Hillside Hospital*, *6*, 131–49.

REXFORD, E. (1966). 'A Survey of the Literature', *A Developmental Approach to Problems of Acting Out*, E. Rexford (ed.). Monographs of the American Academy of Child Psychiatry, No. 1.

RICHFIELD, J. (1954). 'An Analysis of the Concept of Insight', *Psychoanalytic Quarterly*, *23*, 390–408.

RIVIÈRE, J. (1936). 'A Contribution to the Analysis of the Negative Therapeutic Reaction', *International Journal of Psycho-Analysis*, *17*, 304–20.

ROMM, M. (1957). 'Transient Psychotic Episodes During Psychoanalysis', *Journal of the American Psychoanalytic Association*, *5*, 325–41.

ROSEN, J. (1946). 'A Method of Resolving Acute Catatonic Excitement', *Psychiatric Quarterly*, *20*, 183–98.

ROSEN, J. (1953). *Direct Analysis*, New York: Grune & Stratton Inc.

ROSEN, J. (1965). 'The Concept of "Acting-In" ', *Acting Out*, L. Abt and S. Weissman (eds.), New York: Grune & Stratton Inc.

ROSENBLATT, A. D. and THICKSTUN, J. T. (1970). 'A Study of the Concept of Psychic Energy', *International Journal of Psycho-Analysis 51*, 265–78.

ROSENFELD, H. A. (1952). 'Transference Phenomena and Transference-analysis in an Acute Catatonic Schizophrenic Patient', *International Journal of Psycho-Analysis*, *33*, 457–64.

ROSENFELD, H. A. (1954). 'Considerations Regarding the Psychoanalytic Approach to Acute and Chronic Schizophrenia', *International Journal of Psycho-Analysis*, *35*, 135–40.

ROSENFELD, H. A. (1965a). *Psychotic States: A Psychoanalytic Approach*, London: Hogarth Press.

ROSENFELD, H. A. (1965b). 'An Investigation into the Need of Neurotic and Psychotic Patients to Act Out During Analysis', *Psychotic States*, London: Hogarth Press.

ROSENFELD, H. A. (1968). 'Negative Therapeutic Reaction', Unpublished paper.

ROSENFELD, H. A. (1969). 'On the Treatment of Psychotic States by Psycho-Analysis: An Historical Approach', *International Journal of Psycho-Analysis*, *50*, 615–31.

RYCROFT, C. (1958). 'An Enquiry into the Function of Words in the Psycho-analytical Situation', *International Journal of Psycho-Analysis*, *39*, 408–15.

THE PATIENT AND THE ANALYST

RYCROFT, C. (ed.) (1966). *Psychoanalysis Observed*. Harmondsworth: Penguin, 1968.

RYCROFT, C. (1968). *A Critical Dictionary of Psychoanalysis*, London: Thomas Nelson & Sons.

SALZMAN, L. (1960). 'The Negative Therapeutic Reaction', Masserman, J. H. (ed.), *Science and Psychoanalysis, 3,* 303–13.

SANDLER, J. (1959). 'On the Repetition of Early Childhood Relationships in Later Psychosomatic Illness', *The Nature of Stress Disorder*, London: Hutchinson, 1959.

SANDLER, J. (1960a). 'The Background of Safety', *International Journal of Psycho-Analysis, 41,* 352–6.

SANDLER, J. (1960b). 'On the Concept of Superego', *Psychoanalytic Study of the Child, 15,* 128–62.

SANDLER, J. (1968). 'Psychoanalysis: an Introductory Survey', *What is Psychoanalysis*, Jaffe, W. G. (ed.), London: Baillière, Tindall & Cassell, 1–14.

SANDLER, J. (1969). *On the Communication of Psychoanalytic Thought*, Leiden: University Press.

SANDLER, J., DARE, C. and HOLDER, A. (1970a). 'Basic Psychoanalytic Concepts: I. The Extension of Clinical Concepts Outside the Psychoanalytic Situation', *British Journal of Psychiatry, 116,* 551–4.

SANDLER, J., DARE, C. and HOLDER, A. (1970b). 'Basic Psychoanalytic Concepts: III. Transference', *British Journal of Psychiatry, 116,* 667–72.

SANDLER, J., DARE, C. and HOLDER, A. (1970c). 'Basic Psychoanalytic Concepts: VIII. Special Forms of Transference', *British Journal of Psychiatry, 117,* 561–8.

SANDLER, J., DARE, C. and HOLDER, A. (1970d). 'Basic Psychoanalytic Concepts: IX. Working Through', *British Journal of Psychiatry, 117,* 617–21.

SANDLER, J., DARE, C. and HOLDER, A. (1971). 'Basic Psychoanalytic Concepts: X. Interpretations and Other Interventions', *British Journal of Psychiatry, 118,* 53–9.

SANDLER, J., HOLDER, A. and DARE, C. (1970a). 'Basic Psychoanalytic Concepts: II. The Treatment Alliance', *British Journal of Psychiatry. 116,* 555–8.

SANDLER, J., HOLDER, A. and DARE, C. (1970b). 'Basic Psychoanalytic Concepts: IV. Counter-transference', *British Journal of Psychiatry, 117,* 83–8.

SANDLER, J., HOLDER, A. and DARE, C. (1970c). 'Basic Psychoanalytic Concepts: V. Resistance', *British Journal of Psychiatry, 117,* 215–21.

SANDLER, J., HOLDER, A. and DARE, C. (1970d). 'Basic Psychoanalytic Concepts: VI. Acting Out', *British Journal of Psychiatry, 117,* 329–34.

SANDLER, J., HOLDER, A. and DARE, C. (1970e). 'Basic Psychoanalytic

Concepts: VII. The Negative Therapeutic Reaction', *British Journal of Psychiatry*, *117*, 431–5.

SANDLER, J., HOLDER, A., KAWENOKA, M., KENNEDY, H. E. and NEURATH, L. (1969). 'Notes on Some Theoretical and Clinical Aspects of Transference', *International Journal of Psycho-Analysis*, *50*, 633–45.

SANDLER, J., HOLDER, A. and MEERS, D. (1963). 'The Ego Ideal and The Ideal Self', *Psychoanalytic Study of the Child*, *18*, 139–58.

SANDLER, J. and JOFFE, W. G. (1968). 'Psychoanalytic Psychology and Learning Theory', *The Role of Learning in Psychotherapy*, Porter, R. (ed.), London: J. & A. Churchill Ltd.

SANDLER, J. and JOFFE, W. G. (1969). 'Towards a Basic Psychoanalytic Model', *International Journal of Psycho-Analysis*, *50*, 79–90.

SANDLER, J. and JOFFE, W. G. (1970). Discussion of 'Towards a Basic Psychoanalytic Model', *International Journal of Psycho-Analysis*, *51*, 183–93.

SAUL, L. J. (1962). 'The Erotic Transference', *Psychoanalytic Quarterly*, *31*, 54–61.

SCHMALE, H. T. (1966). 'Working Through' (panel report), *Journal of the American Psychoanalytic Association*, *14*, 172–82.

SCHON, D. A. (1963). *The Displacement of Concepts*, London: Tavistock Publications Ltd.

SEARLES, H. F. (1961). 'Phases of Patient-Therapist Interaction in the Psychotherapy of Chronic Schizophrenia', *British Journal of Medical Psychology*, *34*, 160–93.

SEARLES, H. F. (1963). 'Transference Psychosis in the Psychotherapy of Chronic Schizophrenia', *International Journal of Psycho-Analysis*, *44*, 249–81.

SEGAL, H. (1962). 'The Curative Factors in Psycho-Analysis', *International Journal of Psycho-Analysis*, *43*, 212–7.

SEGAL, H. (1964). *Introduction to the Work of Melanie Klein*, London: Wm. Heinemann Ltd.

SHARPE, E. F. (1947). 'The Psycho-analyst', *International Journal of Psycho-Analysis*, *28*, 1–6.

SILVERBERG, W. V. (1955). 'Acting Out Versus Insight: a Problem in Psychoanalytic Technique', *Psychoanalytic Quarterly*, *24*, 527–44.

SPITZ, R. (1956). 'Counter transference: Comments on its Varying Role in the Analytic Situation', *Journal of the American Psychoanalytic Association*, *4*, 256–65.

STERBA, R. (1934). 'The Fate of the Ego in Analytic Therapy', *International Journal of Psycho-Analysis*, *15*, 117–26.

STERBA, R. (1940). 'The Dynamics of the Dissolution of the Transference Resistance', *Psychoanalytic Quarterly*, *9*, 363–79.

STERN, A. (1924). 'On the Counter-transference in Psychoanalysis', *Psychoanalytic Review*, *11*, 166–74.

141

STEWART, W. A. (1963). 'An Inquiry into the Concept of Working Through', *Journal of the American Psychoanalytic Association*, 11, 474–99.

STONE, L. (1961). *The Psychoanalytic Situation*, New York: International Universities Press.

STONE, L. (1967). 'The Psychoanalytic Situation and Transference: Postscript to an Earlier Communication', *Journal of the American Psychoanalytic Association*, 15, 3–58.

STRACHEY, J. (1934). 'The Nature of the Therapeutic Action of Psychoanalysis', *International Journal of Psycho-Analysis*, 15, 127–59.

SULLIVAN, H. S. (1931). 'The Modified Psychoanalytic Treatment of Schizophrenia', *American Journal of Psychiatry*, 11, 519–40.

SZASZ, T. S. (1963). 'The Concept of Transference', *International Journal of Psycho-Analysis*, 44, 432–43.

TARACHOW, S. (1963). *An Introduction to Psychotherapy*, New York: International Universities Press.

TOWER, L. E. (1956). 'Countertransference', *Journal of the American Psychoanalytic Association*, 4, 224–55.

TYSON, R. L. and SANDLER, J. (1971). 'Problems in the Selection of Patients for Psychoanalysis', *British Journal of Medical Psychology*, 44, 211–28.

VALENSTEIN, A. F. (1962). 'The Psycho-Analytic Situation: Affects, Emotional Reliving and Insight in the Psycho-Analytic Process', *International Journal of Psycho-Analysis*, 43, 315–24.

WAELDER, R. (1956). 'Introduction to the Discussion on Problems of Transference', *International Journal of Psycho-Analysis*, 37, 367–8.

WALLERSTEIN, R. S. (1967). 'Reconstruction and Mastery in the Transference Psychosis', *Journal of the American Psychoanalytic Association*, 15, 551–83.

WEXLER, M. (1960). 'Hypotheses Concerning Ego Deficiency in Schizophrenia', *The Out-Patient Treatment of Schizophrenia*, New York: Grune & Stratton Inc.

WINNICOTT, D. W. (1949). 'Hate in the Countertransference', *International Journal of Psycho-Analysis*, 30, 69–74.

WINNICOTT, D. W. (1954). 'Metapsychological and Clinical Aspects of Regression Within the Psychoanalytical Set-up', *Collected Papers: Through Paediatrics to Psycho-Analysis*, London: Tavistock Publications Ltd., 1958.

WINNICOTT, D. W. (1955). 'Clinical Varieties of Transference', *Collected Papers: Through Paediatrics to Psycho-Analysis*, London: Tavistock Publications Ltd., 1958.

WINNICOTT, D. W. (1960). 'Countertransference', *British Journal of Medical Psychology*, 33, 17–21.

WYNNE, L. and SINGER, M. (1963). 'Thought Disorder and Family Relations of Schizophrenics', *Archives of General Psychiatry*, 9, 191–8 and 199–206.

ZELIGS, M. (1957). 'Acting In', *Journal of the American Psychoanalytic Association*, 5, 685–706.

ZETZEL, E. R. (1956). 'Current Concepts of Transference', *International Journal of Psycho-Analysis*, 37, 369–76.

ZILBOORG, G. (1952). 'The Emotional Problem and the Therapeutic Role of Insight', *Psychoanalytic Quarterly*, 21, 1–24.

Index

Haley, J. 56, 60
Hallucination 57, 72, 100
Hammett, van Buren O. 49, 58
Hartmann, H. 11, 19, 29*n*, 77, 97, 102, 107
Hazen, L. 8
Health, flight into 31, 39*n*, 79, 80
Heimann, P. 65, 68
Hernandez, M. 8
Hill, Professor Sir Denis 7, 12, 57, 70
Hinsie, L. E. 116
Hoffer, W. 34*n*, 64, 66
Holder, A. 7*n*, 30, 46, 85*n*, 94
Homosexuality 33, 59, 63, 100
Horney, K. 87, 88, 89, 90, 91
Hypnosis 13, 14, 21, 22, 71, 121
Hypochondriasis, delusional 57
Hysteria 13–14, 21, 70, 71; *See also* Traumatic event
Hysterical character 51*n*

Id 18, 19, 29*n*, 108, 125*n*; resistance 75, 76*n*, 81, 122, 126
Idealization 30
Identification 11, 77
Illness: depressive 87; gain from 74, 75, 79–80, 81, 82, 85; paranoid 87; psychosomatic 100
Insight 35, 53, 59, 115–20; analyst's 63, 66, 68, 69, 117; and working through 123, 126, 127; discussion of term 116; emotional and intellectual 118–19, 123; interpretation and 24, 108–9, 109*n*, 110, 111; resistance to 81; therapy 121
Instinctual drives (impulses): and id resistance 75–6, 122; and superego 82; control and discharge of 15, 16, 18, 19, 29*n*, 59, 86, 122–3, 126; vicissitudes of, 17, 41, 117
Intellectualization 77
Interpretation 23, 62, 127; and other interventions 104–15, 121; and reconstruction 106–7, 125; mutative 112, 113; negative therapeutic reaction and 88, 89, 91; of resistance 33, 74, 106, 112, 113, 122; presumed action of 113–15; rejected 51, 78, 87; timing of 91, 106, 107, 125; transference 26, 42*n*, 43, 58; types of 112–13; use of term 107–10; working through and 27, 123–4

Intervention 23, 75, 92, 121; *See also* Interpretation
Introjection 11
Investment (cathexis) 16, 16*n*, 41, 54
Isaacs, S. 114
Ivimey, M. 90

Jackson, D. D. 56, 60
Janet, P. 13
Jaspers, K. 116
Joffe, W. G. 32, 57, 80, 82, 91, 127
Jung, C. G. 116, 122
Jungian psychology 12*n*

Kaplan, A. 11
Kawenoka, M. 30, 46
Kemper, W. W. 61, 68
Kennedy, H. E. 30, 46
Kepecs, J. G. 40*n*
Kernberg, O. 66
Khan, M. M. R. 58, 78*n*
Klein, M. 32, 43, 50, 100
Köhler, W. 118
Kraepelin, E. 116
Kris, E. 26, 107, 114–15, 118, 125
Kubie, L. S. 118, 119

Laplanche, J. 13
Lewin, B. 90, 91
Libido: and id-resistance 76*n*, 122; displacement of 41; use of term 12*n*, 16
Lidz, T. 56
Limentani, A. 101
Little, M. 49, 54, 58, 65, 67, 68
Loewald, H. W. 27, 125, 125*n*
Loewenstein, R. M. 44, 45, 78, 107, 108–9, 109*n*
Lorand, S. 78

Main, T. F. 69
Martin, A. R. 118
Masochism 75, 80, 85, 88, 89, 90; *See also* Punishment, need for
Meers, D. 85*n*
Meltzer, D. 32, 100
Menninger, K. 27, 34, 105
Mental apparatus: models of 14–15, 18–19, 20, 29*n*, 107
Meynert, T. 13
Mind 13–14; *See also* Mental apparatus
Mishler, E. G. 56
Money-Kyrle, R. E. 67, 68